The Rapture and Left Behind Lies

By Pansy Blackwell

King James Version

God's Warning
and
A Case in Point

Copyright © 2017 Pansy Blackwell

All rights reserved. No part of this book may be reproduced or transmitted in any form or by any means, electronic or mechanical, including photocopying, recording or by any information storage and retrieval system, without permission in writing from the publisher.

Sky Power Press—Keiser, AR
ISBN: 978-0-692-11928-0
Blackwell, Pansy
The Rapture and Left Behind Lies | Pansy Blackwell
Available Formats: eBook | Paperback distribution

About the Author

Pansy Blackwell resides in a farm community, and researches devout Christianity.

The Rapture and Left Behind Lies, is a must-read, offering other opinions, options, and understanding of Christ's second coming. "Holy Bible scriptures have been chosen to point out what will happen, and not what I cannot prove will happen." I could not find a single scripture to call into question, there is a "rapture." Among other things, Jesus taught about his second return to earth, not about a "rapture."

Furthermore, Jesus Christ is the only person to talk about his descent into the world, not John, Paul, or Matthew. These apostles, or prophets lack the authority to do so. Unlike evangelicals of today, they never taught or preached, other than what Jesus Christ instructed. The term "rapture" has nothing at all to do with Christ's second return to the world, if apt for a better name. Since rapture can refer to transport or seized, Jesus did not ascend into heaven with anyone, and He will not be returning to heaven with anyone.

2 Thessalonians 4:13-18, 1 Corinthians 14:51-57, scriptures such as these shouldn't be taken face value alone.

No one but Jesus Christ ever ascended into heaven,

where God is.

In fact, no one was mentioned in the Holy Bible as "raptured."

And to this day, no one has been "raptured."

But that hasn't stopped these "rapture nuts are hard to crack."

True Worshippers of God should get ready for the great tribulation, and not some false hope, and long-shot, like the "rapture."

Chapter One
Tower of Babel

The idea, or, even an attempt to fulfill some sort of "rapture," debacle is nothing new.

Take for instance, the Tower of Babel story in Genesis, 11. Nimrod's objective was to erect a tower to reach into heaven. Genesis 11:4

God was not pleased with the actions of Nimrod and his fellow countrymen.

Genesis 11:5-6 …And now nothing will be refrained from what they imagined to do.

Nimrod and others conceived a way to enter heaven through their own means

A Case In Point: Job 20:6 though his excellency mount up to the heavens, and

His head reach into the clouds

Isaiah 14:12 How are thou fallen from heaven, O Lucifer, son of the morning! How are thou cut down to the ground, which does weaken the nations!

Isaiah 14:13 For thou has said in thine heart, I will ascend into heaven, I will exalt my throne above the stars of God: I will also sit upon the mount of the congregation, in the sides of the north

Isaiah 14:14 I will ascend upon the heights of the clouds; I will be like the most High

Isaiah 14:15 Yet thou shall be brought down to hell, to the sides of the pit

Luke 10:15 and thou Capernaum, exalted into heaven, shall be thrust down to hell

Job 20:6 though his excellency mount up to the heavens, and his head reach into the clouds;

Job 20:7 yet he shall perish forever like his own dung they that seen him shall say, Where is he?

Job 39:27 does the eagle mount up at my command, and make her nest on high?

Obadiah 1:4 Though thou exalt thyself as an eagle, and though thou set thy nest among the stars, thence, will I bring thee down, said the Lord

Habakkuk 20:9 woe to him that covets an evil covetousness to his house, that he may set his nest on high, that he may be delivered from the power of evil

Amos 9:2 though they dig into hell, thence shall mine hand take them; though they climb up to heaven, thence will I bring them down

Jeremiah 51:53 though Babylon mount up to heaven, and though she should fortify the height of her strength, yet from me shall spoilers come unto her, said the Lord

Chapter Two
Enoch and Elijah

Two of the most prolific men that come to mind, when discussing "the rapture," are Enoch and Elijah.

2 Kings 2:11 and Elijah went up by a whirlwind. Elijah went up by a whirlwind, and not "caught up" by a whirlwind.

2 Kings 2:16-17 sons of the prophets urged Elisha to seek for Elijah. A search team set out to find Elijah three days, but found him not.

A Case In Point: Elijah was not ascended into heaven where God's kingdom is. Elisha and sons of the prophets did not witness that occurrence. Instead, they set out to see if Elijah had eventually landed on a mountain top, or some valley. There wouldn't be a ground search, if he had actually entered God's kingdom.

In fact, since Elijah was alive, when he went up in a whirlwind, precludes him from entering God's kingdom.

No one has ever seen God and lived. Exodus 33:20, John 1:18

Enoch, as we are often told, was "raptured," into

heaven where God is, and did not face death on this earth.

However if we read Genesis 5:23 all the days of Enoch were three hundred and sixty five years.

Genesis 5:22 Enoch walked with God after he beget Methuselah three hundred years

Genesis 5:24 and Enoch walked with God; and he was not; for God took him

Hebrews 11:5 by faith Enoch was translated that he should not see death.

Colossians 1:13 who has delivered us from the power of darkness and has translated us into the kingdom of his dear son

Elijah, 2 Kings 2:11 the prophet Elijah was parted from Elisha into heaven. The heaven referred to in this verse, is the heaven, God made in Genesis.

No one knows, when, how, or where, Elijah ended up, that day, he went up by a whirlwind, and eventually died, and finally went to heaven, to God's kingdom, through death.

A Case in Point: Instead, Elijah went to a place called heaven. A firmament of heaven, Genesis 1:1-8 1:20, and fowl fly above the earth

OF NOTE: A whirlwind wouldn't have a strong enough apex to thrust Elijah into heaven. Job 11:8 high as heaven; what can thou do? deeper than hell, what can thou do?

Elijah went up by a whirlwind. And not "caught

up," or "snatched, away,"

2 kings 2:11-12 there appeared a chariot of fire and parted them both asunder; and Elijah went up by a whirlwind into heaven [not the heaven that's seated at God's kingdom]

But rather, the "sky," or a firmament of heaven, as described in Genesis 1:6-8

OF NOTE: Elisha was parted from Elijah, [Elisha was left behind] Elisha was not "unsaved," or "lost." Elisha was not "left behind," nor, was Elisha, "unsaved," or "lost."

OF NOTE: Since Elijah 'went up' to heaven, and was seen by Elisha, and sons of the prophets, and not 'taken up' to heaven. As likewise, Jesus Christ, "and was not seen," as he ascended into heaven. Elijah could still be seen, and he did not ascend into heaven that day.

Enoch and Elijah couldn't be in "rapture," according to standard definition of such an event. Because Jesus Christ wasn't even born, when Enoch and Elijah were on earth. So, that means, Jesus wasn't on earth, at the time, to transport either one of them, from earth to heaven, even if a "rapture," is true.

"Rapture, "believers, also point out, that Elijah 'went up,' without dying.

A Case In Point: Elijah also didn't meet Jesus in the air.

Elijah died somewhere else, at some point and time.

Elijah wasn't "snatched away," "kidnapped," or "seized," "raped," "abducted," assaulted, or other criminal acts, by the whirlwind and chariots, as word origins for "rapture," seem to suggest. Elijah was not forced from earth to heaven.

"Rapture," suggests, that Elijah went up, without warning. When in fact, he and Elisha were talking about his departing. So, Elijah had plenty of warning. 1 Kings 2:5 …knows thou that the Lord will take away thy master from thy head today? And he answered, yea, I know it, hold your peace.

Exodus 33:20, and he said, Thou cannot see my face; for there can no man see my face and live 'No man.' Meaning, not Moses, not Enoch, and Elijah, or any other prophet.

The whole point of a "rapture," is that, somehow, you can by- pass death and suffering, tribulation, and still see God. When in fact, nothing is further from the truth.

"Caught up," doesn't mean "rapture." Caught up is not a "rapture,' word origin. In fact, "rapture," is origin for the word, rape; to take by force.

Ephesians 4:10 he that descended is the same also that ascended up far above all heavens, that he might fill all things.)

A Case In Point: Jesus Christ ascended far above

what Elijah did in the whirlwind. Jesus was taken up into the heaven of heavens, while Elijah went up into a firmament of heaven, in Genesis 1:6-8

Mark 16:19 So then after the Lord had spoken unto them, he was received up into heaven, and sat on the right hand of God

OF NOTE: Enoch, or Elijah, nor any other, apostle, or disciple, such as Philip or John, were 'received' up into heaven, and the two witnesses

Matthew 17:11 Elijah comes, and shall restore all things

Chapter Three
Heaven and Heaven of Heavens

There are two distinct heavens that God made, One, in Genesis 1:6 let there be a firmament in the midst of the waters 1:7 and God made the firmament …the firmament from the waters which were above the firmament, 1:8 and God called the firmament Heaven. 1:20 and fowl fly above the earth in the open firmament of heaven. Two: The Heaven of Heavens, where God's kingdom is. There is a third heaven, where God's kingdom is located, and where Paul was caught up in a vision. The second heaven to include the stars and the heaven.

Genesis 1:14 and God said let there be lights in the firmament of the heaven to divide the day from the night

Genesis 1:17 God set them in the firmament of the heaven to give light upon the earth.

Genesis 1:20 and God said, let the water bring forth abundantly the moving creatures that has life, and fowl that may fly above the earth in the open firmament of heaven.

Genesis 2:4 these are the generations of the heavens and of the earth when they were created, on the day that the Lord made the earth and the heavens

A Case In Point: Heaven of Heavens is too far up in the sky to ascend from the earth. The heavens of heavens is infinite millions of miles upwards. Job 11:8 it is high as heaven; what can thou do? deeper than hell, what can thou do?

Psalms 57:5 be exalted, Oh God, above the heavens

Psalms 79:2 the dead bodies of the servants have they given to be meat unto fowls of the heaven, flesh of saints unto beasts of the earth

Nehemiah 2:4 Then the king said to me, for what does thou make request? So I prayed to the God of heaven

2 Peter 3:10 in which the heavens shall pass away with a great noise, and the elements shall melt with fervent heat

Matthew 13:24 the kingdom of heaven is like unto a man which sowed good seed in his field.

Matthew 13:31 the kingdom of heaven is like unto a grain of mustard seed which a man took and sowed in his field

Matthew 13:33 the kingdom of heaven is like unto leaven…

Matthew 13:44 the kingdom of heaven is like unto treasure hid in a field

Matthew 13:45 the kingdom of heaven is like a

merchant man seeking goodly pearls

Matthew 13:47 the kingdom of heaven is like unto a net, that was cast into the sea

Matthew 18:23 the kingdom of heaven likened unto a certain king ….

Matthew 22:2 the kingdom of heaven is like unto a certain king which made a marriage for his son …….

Matthew 25:1 then shall the kingdom of heaven be likened unto ten virgins…

Matthew 25:14 the kingdom of heaven is like unto a man traveling to a far country, who called his own servants, and delivered unto them goods.

Luke 13:18 what is the kingdom of God like? and whereunto shall I resemble it?

Luke 13:19 it is like a grain of mustard seed, which a man took a cast into a garden…

Luke 13:20 where unto shall I liken the kingdom of God?

Luke 13:21 it is like leaven which a woman took and hid in three measures of meal, till the whole was leavened.

Job 16:19 Behold my witness is in heaven

Job 22:12 Is not God in the height of heaven? And behold the height of the stars, how high they are.

Hebrews 7:26 higher than the heaven of heavens

Ephesians 4:10 He that descended is the same also that ascended up far above all heavens, that he might fill all things.

Daniel 2:37 Thou, O king, are a king of kings: for the God of heaven has given thee a kingdom, power, and strength, and glory

Ezra 7:21 and I, even I Artaxerxes the king do make a decree to all the treasurers which are beyond the river, that whatsoever Ezra, the priest, the scribe of the law of God of heaven shall require of you be done speedily

Ezra 7:23 whatsoever is commanded by the

God of heaven, let it be diligently done for the house of the God of heaven.....

Daniel 7:13 I saw in the night visions, and, behold, one like the Son of man came with the clouds of heaven, and came with the ancient of days, and they brought him near before him.

A Case In Point: Jesus is taken up in the clouds of heaven, whereas, the two witnesses were taken up by a firmament of clouds of heaven.

Psalms 89:6 for who in heaven can be compared to the Lord?

Psalms 104:12 fowl of the heaven have their habitation........

1 Kings 8:27 But will God indeed dwell on the earth, behold, the heaven, and heaven of heavens cannot contain thee how much less this house I have builded?

Deuteronomy 10:14 Behold, the heaven and the

heaven of heavens is the Lord's thy God, the earth also, with all that therein is

Psalm 103:11 For as the heaven is high above the earth, so great is his mercy toward them that fear him

Chapter Four
Rapture Teachings

According to the "rapture," Christians, living and dead, will take flight into the sky, or heaven, and make contact with Jesus Christ. Presumably, Jesus Christ is the transporter, from earth to heaven. All they seem to care about is transportation from earth to heaven. Even if that were true, which it isn't. But are they really ready to meet God in the air? Have they prepared their hearts to meet God, as Ezra did?

Ezra 7:10 For Ezra had prepared his heart to seek the law of the Lord, and to do it, and to teach Israel statues and judgment

1 Peter 4:7 But the end of all things is at hand: be ye therefore sober, and watch unto prayer

1 Timothy 4:1 NOW the Spirit speaks expressly, that in latter times some shall depart from the faith, giving heed to seducing spirits, and doctrines of devils

Romans 10:6 But the righteous which is of faith speak on this wise, Say not in thine heart Who shall ascend into heaven? (that is to bring Christ down from above)

Romans 10:7 or, who shall descend into the deep? (that is, to bring up Christ again from the dead)

A Case In Point: No one departed with Christ, living or dead. In other words, Jesus ascended into heaven alone. Jesus never removed anyone from the earth alive, or dead, and ascended into heaven with them.

No groups, or large number of people ever ascended into heaven together. As did, Jesus Christ. Jesus ascended alone into heaven.

Beginning with the "Millennial Kingdom," Christ to reign for a thousand years prior to the final judgment.

OF NOTE; "Millennial Kingdom," is not found in the Holy Bible,

A Case In Point: immediately after the tribulation of those days shall the sun be darkened and the moon shall not give her light, and the stars shall fall from heaven, and the powers of the heavens shall be shaken Matthew 24:29 And then shall appear the sign of the Son of man in heaven then all the tribes of the earth mourn, and they Shall see the Son of man coming in the clouds of heaven with great glory Matthew 24:30

"True believers," of Jesus Christ, will be transformed into spiritual bodies, in the "rapture," and "taken up," from this earth to be in heaven with God. Non-believers will be "left behind," to face severe tribulation, as the Antichrist takes his place halfway through the seven year period.

But the hour come, and now is, when the true worshippers shall worship the Father, in Spirit and in truth; For the Father seeks such to worship him John 4:23

You must worship the Lord in Spirit and in truth John 4:24

A Case In Point: Saints will go through the great tribulation, along with the "unsaved," or "wicked."

Daniel 7:21 I beheld, the same horn made war with the saints and prevailed against them

Daniel 8:25 …he shall wear out the saints of the most high

I have not found your works perfect before God Revelation 3:2

John 17:15 I pray NOT that thou should take them out of the world, but that thou should keep them from evil. This is case in point.

A Case In Point: Non-Christians, as well as, Christians, Jews, and Saints, will be here on earth during the great tribulation period. Revelation 3:2 Be watchful and strengthen the things which remain, that are ready to die: for I have not found thy works perfect before God. OFF NOTE:

Christians will be 'asleep,' when they meet Christ in the air. The Antichrist will make war with the saints; overcome them Revelation 13:7 it was given him to make war with the saints, and to overcome them; and power was given him over all kindred, and tongues, and nations.

Revelation 17:6 I saw the woman drunken with the blood of the saints, and with the blood of the martyrs of Jesus:

Daniel 7:18 But the saints of the most High God shall take the kingdom and possess the kingdom forever, even forever, and ever

OF NOTE: Daniel 7:18 is consistent with Revelation 20:4, if you reject the beast's mark, and his image, you will live with Christ for a thousand years.

According to this view, non-believers will still come to accept Christ in spite of the church absence. The "new- Christian," will endure extreme persecution to the point of death by beheading. In fact, not only the "new- Christian", will face death, but also, the born-again Christians. All nations, kindred and tongues. The antichrist will not make any specifications.

A Case In Point: The saints have not left the earth, as they cannot, according to John 17:15 I pray Not that thou take them out of the world…. In fact, the "true- Christians," are still on earth during the great tribulation, and in much of the book of Revelation.

Revelation 18:24 And in her was found the blood of the prophets, and of saints, and of all that were slain upon the earth. The "new- Christians," blasphemed God and did not repent of their sins and to give him glory. Revelation 2:20

Notwithstanding I have a few things against thee, because thou suffers that woman Jezebel, which calls herself a prophetess, to teach and seduce my servants to commit fornication, and to eat things sacrificed with idols.

Revelation 2:21 And I gave her space to repent of her fornication, and she repented not

Revelation 9:20 The rest of the men which were not killed by these plagues yet repented not of the works of their hands, that they should not worship devils, and idols of gold, and silver and brass, and stone and of wood: which neither can see, nor hear, nor walk

Revelation 9:21 neither repented they of their murders, nor of their sorceries, nor of their fornication, nor of their thefts 17:3.

Revelation 16:9 And the men scorched with great heat, and blasphemed the name of God, which had power over all these plagues: and they repented NOT to give him glory.

Revelation 16:11 And they blasphemed the God of heaven and repented not of their pains, sores, and repented not of their deeds

Revelation 16:21 and men blasphemed God because of the plague of hail

Revelation 17:3 I saw a woman upon a scarlet colored beast, full of names of blasphemy, having seven heads and ten horns.

OF NOTE: Nowhere in Revelation, says that, "the non-Christians, repented of their sins, and will accept Christ, and be forgiven of their sins."

Mid-Tribulation, or "Mid-Trib," believes, Christians from the earth will be with God in heaven, during the middle of the seven year period of tribulation.

OF NOTE: Saints are in Revelation 20, at the end of the great tribulation. And again, John 17:15 I pray NOT that thou take them out of the world.....

A Case In Point: Saints, "Christians," will not be "taken up," or "removed, "or even leave the earth, during the coming great tribulation period. John 17:15 precludes this fact.

John prays to not take them out of the world, but to keep them from evil. The Saints, and Christians, as well as, the unsaved, are in the midst of the great tribulation, throughout most of the book of Revelation.

Revelation 18:24 And in her was found the blood of the prophets, and of saints, and all that was slain upon the earth.

Revelation 19:11 and I saw heaven opened and behold a white horse; and he that sat upon him was called Faithful and True, and in righteousness he does judge and make war.

Revelation 20:4 I saw the souls of them beheaded for the witness of Jesus, and for the word of God, which had not worshipped the beast or his image, neither had received the mark upon their foreheads, or in their hands; and they lived and reigned with Christ a thousand years.

Revelation 20:9 And they went up on the breath of the earth and compassed the camp of the saints about, and fire came down from heaven and devoured them.

Revelation 22:7, and 22:12, Behold I come quickly

OF NOTE: When Christ returns in Revelation 19, and 22, he sets up Revelation 3:2, which sets up 1 Thessalonians 4:13-17 and Luke 9:27

OF NOTE; All will die prior the meeting with Christ in the air.

Christians, and other individuals, which believe in a

"rapture," have upheld these bible scriptures to support their beliefs.

1 Timothy 4:1 NOW the spirit speaks expressly, that in the latter times some shall depart from the faith, giving heed to seducing spirits, and doctrines of devils

Matthew 16:27 the Son of man shall come in his glory of his Father and with his angels, and he shall reward every man according to his works.

A Case In Point: the verse is referring to Christ's second return to earth. Which of course, is after the great tribulation, and not before. Matthew 24:29-30.

Matthew 24:30 then shall appear the sign of the Son of man in heaven; and then shall all the tribes of the earth mourn, and they shall see the Son of man coming in the clouds of heaven with power and great glory.

Matthew 25:31-32 When the Son of man shall come in his glory, then shall he sit upon the throne of his glory.

Matthew 25:32 and before him shall be gathered all nations …

Mark 12:18 Then come the Sadducees which say there is no resurrection

Luke 9:27 then came to him certain of the Sadducees, which deny there is any resurrection; and they asked him:

Mark 12:19 if a brother die, and leave his brother behind him, and have no children….

Mark 12:20 now there were seven brethren: and the first took a wife, dying left no seed

Mark 12:21 and the second took her and died, neither left he any seed….

Mark 12:22 and the seven had her and left no seed….

Mark 12:23 in the resurrection therefore, when they shall rise, whose wife will she be of them? for the seven had her to wife

Mark 12:24 Jesus answering them: Do not ye therefore err because ye know not the scriptures

Mark 12:25 for when they shall rise from the dead, they neither marry, nor are given in marriage, nor are given in marriage, but are as the angels which are in heaven

Mark 12:26 and as touching the dead they rise:

Mark 12:27 He is not the God of the dead, but the God of the living: ye therefore do greatly err

Mark 12:28 and one of the scribes came having heard them reasoning together and perceiving…

Mark 12:29 Jesus answered: the first of all the commandments is Hear O Israel; The Lord our God is one Lord

A Case In Point: If one would be hard-pressed to know, when the Son of man comes.

The answer: After the great tribulation, and not before. Those that died in Christ shall rise first. Some will rise to eternal life, others to eternal damnation. Not only do they also err because, they know not the scriptures, but rather, they won't admit the scriptures.

Acts 24:15 And have hope toward God, which they themselves also allow, there shall be a resurrection of the dead, both of just and unjust

Mark 13:24 But in those days after that the tribulation the sun shall be darkened…

Mark 13:26 then shall they see the Son of man coming in the clouds with great power and glory

Luke 17:26 as it was in the days of Noe, so shall it also be in the days of the Son of man

Luke 17:27 the did eat they drank they married wives, they were given in marriage, until the day that Noe entered into the ark, and the flood came and destroyed them all

Luke 17:28 Likewise also as it was in the days of Lot; they did eat they drank, they bought they sold, they planted, they build.

Luke 17:29 but the same day Lot went out of Sodom it rained fire and brimstone from heaven, and destroyed them all

Luke 17:30 even thus shall it be in the day when the Son of man is revealed

Luke 17:31 in that day which he shall be upon the housetop let him not come down and take it away: and he that is in the field, let him likewise not return back

Luke 17:32 Remember Lot's wife

Luke 17:33 whosoever shall seek to save his life shall lose it; and whosoever shall save his life shall preserve it

Luke 17:34 I tell you in that night there shall be two men in a bed; the one shall be taken the other shall be left

Luke 17:35 two women shall be grinding

together; the one shall be taken the other left

Luke 17:36 Two men shall be in the field: The one shall be taken the other left

A Case In Point: Matthew 24:23 if any man say unto you, Lo, here is Christ, or there, believe it not.

Matthew 24:26 Behold he is in the dessert, go not forth, Behold, he is in the secret chambers, believe it not.

OF NOTE: Jesus isn't coming "any moment now." Christ isn't returning before the great tribulation.

A Case In Point: Lot wasn't taken to heaven during the days of Sodom and Gomorrah. Lot's wife was destroyed. In Luke 17:34 the man that was taken, endured eternal damnation in that night. There shall be weeping and gnashing of teeth. Luke 17:35 the two women grinding together; the one that was taken also went to hell. Likewise, Luke 17:36 the one taken in the field, lost his soul.

Matthew 25:30 Cast the unprofitable servant into outer darkness there shall be weeping and gnashing of teeth.

John 5:21 for as the Father raises up the dead and quickens them; even so the son quickens whom he will

John 5:28 marvel not at this for the hour is coming in the which all that are in the graves shall hear his voice

John 5:29 and shall come forth they that have done good unto the resurrection of life; and they that have done evil unto the resurrection of damnation.

OF NOTE: The verse is referring to the first and second resurrection explained in Revelation 20:5-6.

A Case In Point: None will be returning to heaven with Jesus Christ, when he returns. The righteous have died, and gone to heaven, even before Christ returns, in 1 Thessalonians 4:13-17

Both scriptures, John 5:21, and John 5:28, are in contradiction to support a "rapture." The dead are not "snatched," or "seized." No one in the Holy Bible was forcibly removed from the earth to enter heaven

1 Corinthians 6:14 and God has raised up the Lord and will also raise us up by his own power.

1 Corinthians 15:12 now if Christ be preached that he rose from the dead, how say some among you there is no resurrection of the dead.

A Case In Pont: Christians will be raised in the first resurrection. The non-Christians that are "left behind," are the lost souls, eternally separated from God, are in the second resurrection. This is called the second death

Revelation 20:5 but the rest of the dead lived not again until the thousand years were finished. This is the first resurrection.

Revelation 20:6 blessed and holy is he that has part in the first resurrection: on search the second death have no power, but they shall be priests of God and of Christ and shall reign with him a thousand years.

OF NOTE; in the first resurrection, are the Christians which return with Christ, to meet those, of whom, are 'alive and remain,' 1 Thessalonians 4:13-17

A Case In Point: The non-Christians that are "left behind," most likely went to hell, are in the second resurrection. Revelation 20:5-6, 20:14, 21:8

1 Corinthians 15:13 but if there be no resurrection of the dead, then is Christ not risen

1 Corinthians 15:14 And if Christ be not risen, then is our preaching vain, and your faith is also vain

1 Corinthians 15:15 yea and we are found false witnesses of God, because we are testified of God that he raised up Christ: whom he raised not up, so be that the dead raise not

1 Corinthians 15:16 For if the dead rise not, then is not Christ raised

Hebrews 11:35 women received their dead raise to life again: and others were tortured, not accepting deliverance; that they might obtain a better resurrection

A Case In Point: The dead are raised

incorruptible

1 Corinthians 15:17 And if Christ be not raised, your faith is raised, your faith is vain; ye are yet in your sins

1 Corinthians 15:18 Then they also which are fallen asleep Christ are perished

1 Corinthians 15:19 if in this life only we have hope in Christ we are of all men most miserable

Ephesians 5:14 why he said, Arise ye that sleep, and arise from the dead and Christ shall give thee light

1 Corinthians 15:20 But now is Christ risen from the dead, and become the first fruits of them that slept

1 Corinthians 15:21 For since by man come death, by man come also the resurrection of the dead

1 Corinthians 15:22 For as in Adam all men die, even so in Christ shall all be made alive

1 Corinthians 15:23 But every man in his own order: Christ the first fruits; afterward they that are Christ's at his coming

1 Corinthians 15:24 Then come the end when he shall have delivered up the kingdom of God, even the Father when he put down all rule and all authority and power

1 Corinthians 15:25 For he must reign till he put all enemies under his feet

1 Corinthians 15:26 The last enemy that shall be

destroyed is death

1 Corinthians 15:27 For he has put all things under his feet…

1 Corinthians 15:28 When all things shall be subdued unto him then shall the Son also himself be subject unto him that put all things under him, that God may be all in all

1 Corinthians 15:29 Else what shall they do which are baptized for the dead, if the dead rise not at all? Why are they then baptized for the dead

1 Corinthians 15:30 And why stand we in jeopardy every hour?

1 Corinthians 15:31 I protest by your rejoicing which I have in Christ Jesus our Lord, I die daily

1 Corinthians 15:32 if after the manner of men I have fought with beasts of Ephesus, what advantage if the dead rise not? Let us eat and drink for tomorrow we die

A Case In Point: The term used in each of these scriptures is, either, 'rise,' or 'raise', not "rapture." Nowhere in the New Testament was Jesus Christ associated with the term "rapture."

Since "rapture," words and origins are criminal, why would Christ do something that is unlawful? To "snatch," "seize," "carry off," "rape," are all assaults. These are all word origins for a "rapture."

In the foregoing scriptures, these individuals are already in heaven, in the first place, if they died in

Christ. They have no biblical reason to meet Jesus in the air, when, God has already raised them from the dead. The Christians alive and remain, will go on to meet Christ in the air, after they are ready to die. Revelation 3:2, 1 Corinthians 15:52, Luke 9:27, You cannot take 1 Thessalonians 4:13-17 at face value.

OF NOTE; For instance, is your heart ready to meet God in the air, as Ezra, prepared his?

Ezra 7:10 For Ezra had prepared his heart to seek the law of the Lord, and to do it, and to teach Israel statues and judgment

1 Peter 4:7 But the end of all things is at hand: be ye therefore sober, and watch unto prayer

Philippians 3:20 for our conversation is in heaven; from whence we look for our Savior; The Lord Jesus Christ

Philippians 3:21 who shall change our vile body, that it may be fashioned like unto his glorious body according to the working whereby he is able to subdue all things unto himself

Colossians 3:4 When Christ, who is our life, shall appear with him in glory

A Case In Point: the "rapture," term, appears in neither of these scriptures

2 Peter 3:8 but beloved be not ignorant of this one thing, one day is with the Lord as a thousand years, and a thousand years as one day

2 Peter 3:9 the Lord is no slack concerning his

promise as some men count slackness: but is longsuffering to us-ward, not willing that any should perish, but that all should come to repentance

2 Peter 3:10 but the day of the Lord will come as a thief in the night; in the which the heavens shall pass away with great noise, and the elements shall melt with fervent heat, the earth also and the works that are in therein shall be burned up

The 'day,' shall come. And not Jesus himself.

Revelation 1:7 behold he comes with clouds; and every eye shall see him, and they also which pierced him: and all kindred of the earth shall wail because of him. Even so Amen.

A Case In Point: John 8:21 I go my way and you shall seek me, and shall die in your sins, whither I go, you cannot come.

OF NOTE; for those of you to continue to believe in a so-called rapture, you could very well end up in hell. You cannot ascend into heaven with Jesus Christ, "living or dead." A belief in a "rapture, "is out of the realm of God.

John 13:26 whither I go, thou cannot follow me now, but thou shall follow me afterwards.

OF NOTE: apostles did not ascend into heaven with Jesus Christ. John 21:23 Jesus entered and left this world alone.

Chapter Five
Rapture Beliefs

Some "rapture," enthusiasts, insist that Christians, living or dead, will rise into the sky, and be transported from the earth to heaven, to "join," Christ in the air.

OF NOTE: Are the rapture people ready to meet God in the air? Have they really prepared their hearts, as Ezra did?

Ezra 7:10 For Ezra had prepared his heart to seek the law of the Lord, and to do it, and to teach Israel statues and judgments

1 Peter 4:7 But the end of all things is at hand: be ye therefore sober, and watch unto prayer

A Case In Point: this belief gives rise to the beliefs of mystics, trances, ambiences, all of which, are not Christian, and unacceptable behavior towards God.

Romans 10:6 But the righteous which is of faith speak on the wise, Say not in thine heart who shall ascend into heaven? (that is to bring Christ down from above)

Romans 10:7 or, who shall descend into the deep? (that is, to bring up Christ again from the dead)

A Case In Point: 2 Thessalonians 2:11 for this cause God shall send strong delusion on them that should believe a lie.

OF NOTE: God called it what it is, a lie.

A Case In Point: the word "sky," says it all.

"Sky," is the term "heaven." Genesis 1:1-8

"Disappear," "suddenly without warning, from the earth," in a twinkling of an eye.

OF NOTE: No where did the verse mention "disappearing acts, or "suddenly without warning."

1 Peter 4:5 where shall give account to him to judge the quick and the dead

A Case In Point: In order for Christians to ascend into heaven the same method, Jesus Christ did, Christians would have to die, and be raised again, to life-form, on earth, the same as, Jesus died and rose again, and was seen three times by his disciples, and Mary Magdalene.

OF NOTE: apparently, "rapture," believers don't believe that anyone is in heaven. Only the Christians that 'remain' will meet Christ in the air. The Christian - dead are already in heaven. They are the 'reward,' Christ was talking about, when he inferred, he was returning with them. The second-resurrected dead, will not meet God in the air. Because they are eternally separated from God.

The "rapture," is a mystical, delusional belief that the Christians will be transported to a heavenly realm, through Jesus Christ, and he will somehow be the transport. They believe, they will not endure suffering or tribulation.

The "rapture," is on par with the queen of heaven, Jeremiah 7:18 the children gather wood, and the fathers kindle the fire, and the women knead their dough, to make cakes to the queen of heaven, and to pour out drink offerings to other gods, that they may provoke me to anger

Jeremiah 7:19 Do they provoke me to anger? Said the Lord, do they not provoke themselves to the confusion of their own faces?

A Case In Point: 2 Thessalonians 2:11 for this cause God shall send strong delusion on them that should believe a lie.

Pre-Tribulation Rapture, the rapture will occur before not during the Second Coming with or without extended tribulation period. John ascends to heaven.

And to support this theory, is Revelation 4:1-2, AFTER that I looked a door opened to heaven: the first voice I heard was it were a trumpet talking with me; which said Come up hither, and I must show these things which must be hereafter 1:2 and immediately I was in the spirit; and behold a throne was set in heaven, and one sat on the throne

Daniel 9:27 And he shall confirm the covenant with many for one week: and in the midst of the week he shall cause the sacrifice and oblation to cease.......

A Case In Point: Jesus is not returning to earth to fulfill Daniel 9:24-27

A Case In Point: Christ must remain in heaven until all prophesy has been fulfilled Acts 3:20-21 and he shall send Jesus Christ, which before was preached unto you. Acts 3:21 when the heaven must receive until the time of restitution all things God has spoken by the mouth of all his holy prophets since he world began

Revelation 7:14 And I said unto him, Sir, thou knows. And he said unto me, These are they which came out of great tribulation, and have washed their robes, and made them white in the blood of the Lamb.

A Case In Point: Revelation 7:14 says, that, the saints will not only go through the great tribulation, when it happens, but, they will come out "sanctified," or filled with "the Holy Spirit," from their endurance, and sufferings.

OF NOTE: Revelation 3:10 Because thou has kept the word of my patience. I will also keep thee from the hour of temptation which will come upon all the world, to try them that dwell upon all the earth.

OF NOTE: All kindred, nations and tongues, will be affected, by the antichrist. Revelation 3:10

Revelation 11:11 and after three days in a half the Spirit of life from God entered into them, and they stood upon their feet; and great fear fell upon all them which saw them

Revelation 11:12 I heard a great voice from heaven saying unto them, Come up hither. And they ascended up to heaven in a cloud; and their enemies beheld them.

A Case In Point: again, not the kingdom of God, the two witnesses ascended into, but rather, a firmament of heaven, the 'sky,' or where fowls fly around in. Their enemies could not see above the clouds, to see the two witnesses, go to the place where God sits on the throne.

That Heaven is infinite, millions of miles away. The two witnesses did not ascend into Heaven, the same way, Jesus Christ ascended behind the clouds, out of sight.

Revelation 16:17 and the seventh angel poured out his vial into the air; and there came a great voice out of the temple of heaven, from the throne, saying, It is done

Revelation 16:18 and there were voices, and thunders, and lightnings, and there was a great earthquake such as was not since men were upon the earth, so mighty and earthquake, and so great

Revelation 16:19 And the great city was divided into three parts, and the cities of the nations fell; and great Babylon came into remembrance before God, to give her the cup of the wine of fierceness of his wrath.

Revelation 16:20 And every island fled away, and the mountains were not found.

Revelation 16:21 And there fell upon men a great hail out of heaven, every stone about the weight of a talent: and men blasphemed God because of the plague of the hail; for the plague thereof was exceeding great.

A Case In Point: No one is "raptured," in these scriptures, either, living or dead. In fact, "The Left Behind," heresy, is about non-Christians, finally coming to Christ, and repenting of their sins. But, Revelation 16:21 and men blasphemed God because of the plague, disputes that.

Matthew 24:40 then shall the two be in the field; the one taken, the other left.

Matthew 25:41 the two women grinding at the mill; and the one shall be taken, and the other left.

Of NOTE: The "one taken," is raised in the second resurrection Revelation 20:5-6,20:14,21:8

A Case In Point: in each of these scriptures, the ones 'taken,' are the ones, lost to all eternity, and Not the ones "left behind." The ones that are left behind, are the saved ones, and were not separated from God.

Matthew 24:50 The Lord of that servant shall come in a day when he look not for him, and in an hour that he is not aware of

Matthew 24:51 and shall cut him asunder, appoint him his portion with the hypocrites; there shall be weeping and gnashing of teeth

OF NOTE; The second resurrection Revelation 20:6 the has no power and is the Lake of Fire.

Elisha, was left behind, when Elijah went up in a whirlwind. Elisha was not "unsaved," and therefore, was not, "left behind," in that sense, and raised in the second resurrection.

John 14:1-3 LET not your heart be troubled: ye believe in God, believe also in me.

John 14:2 in my Father's house are many mansions if it were not so, I would have told you, I go to prepare a place for you.

John 14:3 and if I go and prepare a place for you, I will come again and receive you unto myself, that where I am, there ye may be also.

A Case In Point: John 13:33 Little Children, yet a little while I am with you, Ye shall seek me; I said unto the Jews, Wither I go you cannot come; so now I say unto you; so now I say unto you

John 14:6 I am the way the truth and the life; no man come unto the Father, but by me. John 16:10 of righteousness if go to my Father and you see me no more

John 16:16 yet in a little while and ye shall not see me: in a little while ye shall see me, because I go to the Father

John 17:15 I pray not that thou should take them out of the world, that thou should keep them from evil.

Acts 1:9 And when he had spoken these things, while they beheld, he was taken up; and a cloud received him out of their sight

Acts 1:10 And while they looked steadfastly toward heaven as he went up, behold, two men stood by them in white apparel

Acts 1:11 Which also said, Ye men of Galilee, why stand ye gazing up into heaven? this same Jesus which is taken up from you into heaven so shall come in like manner as ye have seen him go into heaven

OF NOTE; No one, not even the apostles, ascended to heaven with Jesus Christ

1 Corinthians 15:51 Behold, I show you mystery; we shall not all sleep, but we shall all be changed.

A Case In Point: Revelation 3:2 Be watchful and strengthen the things which REMAIN, that are ready to DIE; because I have not found thy works perfect before God.

1 Corinthians 15:52 in a moment in the twinkling of an eye, at the last trump: for the

trumpet shall sound, and the dead shall be raised incorruptible, and we shall be changed.

A Case In Point: Revelations 8:2 and, I saw the seven angels which stood before God; and to them were given seven trumpets 8:6 and the seven angels which had the seven trumpets prepared themselves to sound. OF NOTE; It isn't until Revelation 10:7 and the seventh angel sounded: …..

A Case In Point: The church, depending upon which church, the "rapture," people are referring to, didn't happen. There are seven trumpets to sound, not one.

No church was taken out of the world yet, at the first trumpet.

There were still six more trumpets for the angels to sound.

Acts 8:39 and when they were come up out of the water, the Spirit of the Lord caught away Philip, that the eunuch saw him no more: and he went on his way rejoicing.

A Case In Point: Acts 8:40 But Philip was found at Azotus: and passing through he preached in all the cities, till he came to Caesarea OF NOTE; Philip never left the earth. Philip did not disappear suddenly from earth in a twinkling of an eye. Philip was not ascended into heaven of heavens. "caught away," is not a word origin for a "rapture," Philip was caught up into the sky, or the firmament of heaven. Philip was 'caught away,' not "caught up."

In 'twinkling of an eye,' no one will be alive, when saints meet Christ in the air, not join, him in the air.

Christians, "dead or alive," are not returning with Jesus Christ, when he returns a second time. He said to, 'meet,' him in the air, not returning, or transporting. And upon this meeting, Christians will have to be asleep, as do the ones, Christ brings with him from the first resurrection.

2 Corinthians 12:2 I knew a man in Christ fourteen years ago, (whether in body I cannot tell; or whether out of the body: God knows)

Such as one caught up to the third heaven.

2 Corinthians 12:3 And I know such a man whether in the body, or out of the body, I cannot tell: (God knows)

2 Corinthians 12:4 How that he was caught up into Paradise, and heard unspeakable words, which is not lawful for a man to utter.

A Case In Point: Paul was 'caught away,' not "snatched up," "seized," or "raped," nor anything else of forcibly removal. "Caught away," is not a word origin for a "rapture," And besides, Paul was 'caught up,' in a vision, so, it's moot point, anyways.

Chapter Six
Sinners, Saints, Cannot Ascend to Heaven

If there was ever a single reason, as to why, the Saints will go through the great tribulation, the one word that comes to mind is sin. Sin is the explanation why, Christians cannot return with the Lord in the air, dead or alive. Those that died in Christ will meet the Lord in the air. Christ never transported anyone to heaven. Therefore saints are sinners, hypocrites, Pharisees, Sadducees, and Chief Priests. They can talk about meeting God in the air, all they want to, and yet, they have not prepared their hearts to meet God in the air, as Ezra did.

Matthew 3:7 for when he saw many of the Pharisees and Sadducees come to his baptism, he said, unto them, O generation of vipers, who has warned you to flee from the wrath to come?

Ezra 7:10 For Ezra had prepared his heart to seek the law of the Lord, and to do it, and to teach Israel statues and judgment

1 Peter 4:7 But the end of all things is at hand: be ye therefore sober, and watch unto prayer

Romans 5:12 Wherefore, as by one man entered into the world, and death by sin; and do death passed upon all men

OF NOTE: Adam is the first man on record to have committed sin, and died because of it.

Romans 3:23 For all have sinned and come short of the glory of God

Romans 5:2 wherefore by one man entered into the world and death by sin and so death passed upon all men: for that all have sinned.

Romans 5:3 and not only so, but we glory in tribulations also: knowing that tribulation works patience

Romans 5:12 wherefore, as by one man sin entered into the world, and death by sin; and so death passed upon all men, and they all have sinned.

Romans 5:19 for as by one man's disobedience many were made sinners, so by the obedience of one shall many be made righteous

Daniel 9:5 we have sinned, and have committed iniquity, and have done wickedly, and have rebelled, even by departing from the precepts

Romans 5:21 sin has reigned unto death, even so might grace reign through righteousness unto eternal life by Jesus Christ our Lord

1 John 1:8 if we say we have no sin, we deceive ourselves, and the truth is not in us

1 John 1:10 if we say we have no sinned, we make him a liar, and his word is not in us

1 John 3:5 and ye know that he was manifested to take away our sins, and in him is no sin.

1 John 3:9 whosoever is born of God does not commit sin; for his seed remains in him: and he cannot sin, because he is born of God

John 3:13 And no man has ascended up to heaven, but he that came down from heaven, even the Son of man which is from heaven

1 John 5:16 if any man see his brother sins a sin which is not unto death, he shall ask, and he shall give, and he shall give him life for them that sin not unto death. There is a sin unto death: I do not say he shall pray for it

1 John 5:17 all unrighteousness is sin: and there is a sin not unto death

A Case In Pont: we have all heard them say, 'there is no big sin, or a little sin," meaning, "they all are the same." Well, this verse disproves that saying. Not all "sins," are alike.

John 8:23 ye are from beneath; I am from above: ye are of this world; I am not of this world.

John 8:34 verily, verily I say unto you, Whosoever commits sin is the servant of sin

Romans 6:7 for he that is dead is freed from sin

Romans 6:8 now if we believe we be dead with Christ, we believe we shall also live with him

Romans 6:9 knowing that Christ raised from the dead dies no more; death has no more dominion over him

Romans 6:10 For in that he died, he died unto sin once: but on that he lived, he lives unto sin, but alive unto God through Jesus Christ our Lord

Romans 6:23 for the wages of sin is death

Romans 6:6 knowing that that our old man is crucified with him, that the body of sin might be destroyed, that henceforth we should not serve sin

Romans 13:13 neither yield your members as instruments of unrighteousness unto sin: but yield yourselves unto God as those that are alive from the dead

Romans 13:12 let not sin therefore reign in your mortal body, that ye should obey it in the lusts thereof

1 Peter 22 who died no sin neither guile found in his mouth

Hebrews 3:17 but with whom was he grieved forty years? Was it not with them that had sinned, who carcasses fell in the wilderness?

Acts 2:38 then Peter said unto them Repent and be baptized every one of you in the name of Jesus Christ for the remission of sins, and shall receive the gift of the Holy Ghost

1 Peter 4:18 if the righteous scarcely be saved, where shall the ungodly and the sinner appear?

Luke 3:7 O generation of vipers, who has warned you of the wrath to come?

Luke 9:31 For we know that God hears not sinners, but any man be a worshipper of God, and does his will, him he hears

1 John 3:5 ye know that he was manifested to take away our sins, and in him is no sin

Isaiah 26:10 let favor be showed unto the wicked, yet will he not learn righteousness; in the land of uprightness; in the land of uprightness, will he deal unjustly, and will not behold the majesty of the Lord

Isaiah 26:14 They are dead, they shall not rise: therefore has thou visited and destroyed them, and made all their memory to perish

John 5:29 and shall come forth they that have done good unto the resurrection of life, and they that have done evil unto the resurrection of damnation

OF NOTE: Isaiah 26:14 is referring to the wicked in the previous verse, 26:10. The second death has no power, Revelation 20:5-6, 20:14, 21:8.

Chapter Seven
1 Thessalonians 4:13-17

1 Thessalonians 4:17 is one of the most often-used bible scriptures to support a "rapture" theory. This verse is strongly about the first and second resurrection, and the day of judgment, and second coming of Jesus Christ

The saved- dead in the first resurrection are in heaven with Jesus Christ. The 'dead in Christ, are the 'saved,' he will bring back with him. The unsaved dead, not included in the first resurrection, or, the non-Christians, are in the second resurrection, which has no power. Revelation 20:5-6, 20:14, and 21:8 These non-Christians, or, the unsaved, wicked, are presently in hell, to be judged. This is the second death, which has no power, and is the Lake of Fire

Ezra 7:10 For Ezra had prepared his heart to seek the law of the Lord, and to do it, and to teach Israel statues and judgment

OF NOTE: prior to his coming, are the saints prepared in their hearts to meet God

1 Thessalonians 5:6 But let us not sleep as others do, but let us watch and be sober

1 Peter 4:7 But the end of all things is at hand: be ye therefore sober, and watch unto prayer

1 Corinthians 15:42 so is the resurrection of the dead. It is given in corruption; it is raised in incorruption

Luke 21:36 Watch ye therefore, and pray always, that ye may be accounted worthy to escape all these things, and to stand before the Son of man

Daniel 12:2 and many of them that sleep in the dust of the earth shall awake, some to everlasting life, some to shame and everlasting contempt

Romans 10:6 But the righteous which is of faith speak on the wise, say not in thine heart Who shall ascend into heaven? (that is to bring Christ down from above.)

Luke 9:27 then came to him certain of the Sadducees, which deny there is any resurrection; and they asked him:

Ephesians 5:14 why he said, Arise ye that sleep, and arise from the dead and Christ……

Revelation 20:6 Blessed and holy is he that has part in the first resurrection: as such the second death has no power, but they shall be priests of God, and of Christ, and shall reign a thousand years

John 5:21 for as the Father raises up the dead and quickens them! Even as the son quickens whom he will

John 5:29 and shall come forth, they that have

done good, unto the resurrection of life; and they that have done evil, unto the resurrection of damnation

Acts 4:1 and as they spoke unto the people, the priests, and captains of the

temple, and Sadducees came upon them

Acts 4;2 being grieved that they taught the people, and preached through Jesus the resurrection from the dead.

Acts 24:15 there shall be a resurrection of the dead both of the just and the unjust

1 Corinthians 6:14 And God has both raised up the Lord, and will also raise up us by his own power

A Case In Point: Never mind that 1 Thessalonians, is apostle Paul talking about Christians, which have died in Christ, and have gone on to be in heaven. And not about ascension, or any other transport.

Romans 10:9 that if thou shall confess with thy mouth, the Lord Jesus and shall believe on him with thine heart, thou shall be saved

Matthew 27:52 And the graves were open, and many bodies of the saints which slept arose

Matthew 27:53 And came out of the graves of the resurrection, and went into the holy city, and appeared unto many

1 Thessalonians 4:13 But I would not have you

ignorant, brethren, concerning them which are asleep in Jesus will God bring with him

Revelation 3:2 be watchful and strengthen the things which remain, that they are ready to die: for I have not found thy works perfect before God

2 Timothy 4:1 I charge you therefore before God and the Lord Jesus Christ who shall judge the quick and the dead at his appearing and his kingdom

Revelation 14:13 and I heard a voice from heaven saying unto me, write, Blessed are the dead which die in the Lord from henceforth: yea, said the Spirit they may rest from their labors; and their works do follow them

A Case In Point: Christ will bring with him the Christians that are dead in Christ, of which are the 'asleep.' Those which died and raised up in the first resurrection

1 Thessalonians 4:16 For the Lord himself shall descend from heaven with a shout, with the voice of the archangel, and with voice of God: and the dead in Christ shall rise first

1 Thessalonians 4:14 For if we believe that God rose and died again, even so them also which sleep in Jesus will God bring with him

1 Thessalonians 4:15 for this we say unto you by the word of the Lord, that we which are alive and remain unto the coming of the Lord shall not prevent them which are asleep

Philippians 1:21 For to me is live in Christ, and to die is gain

1 Corinthians 15:18 they also which are fallen asleep in Christ are perished

OF NOTE; All the faith, guidance, love for Christ and God, are gone in the Christian that cannot awake They lost their first love.

A Case In Point: 'the alive and remain,' will be like the ones, which are 'asleep,' in Jesus, before they meet God in the air. Those that are "asleep," God will bring back with him, not take away from the earth.

The dead, still left on the earth, are in the second death, and resurrection. These are the unsaved, and raised corruptible.

The non-Christians, or the wicked, that are "left behind,' will be eternally separated from God, in the second resurrection.

1 Corinthians 15:52 in a moment, in a twinkling of an eye, at the last trump, for the trumpet shall sound. And the dead shall be raised incorruptible, and we shall all be changed.

Hebrews 9:27 it is appointed unto me once to die, after that the judgment

Romans 2:16 In the day, when God shall judge the secrets of men, by Jesus Christ, according to my gospel

OF NOTE: the 'change,' in this scripture, means

to die. see, Revelation 3:2

Luke 9:27 then certain of the Sadducees, which deny there is any resurrection; and they asked him

Ephesians 5:14 why, he said, awake ye out of the sleep, arise ye from the dead and Christ shall give thee light

Revelation 20:5-6 Second death has no power.

Revelation 20:14 and death and hell cast into the Lake of Fire, that is the second death

1 Thessalonians 4:16 For the Lord himself shall descend from heaven with a shout, with the voice of the archangel, and with the trump of God and the dead in Christ shall rise first:

Revelation 3:2 Be watchful and strengthen the things which remain, that are ready to die: for I have not found thy works perfect before God

2 Timothy 4:1 I charge you therefore before God, and the Lord Jesus Christ, who shall judge the quick and the dead at his appearing in his kingdom

Revelations 21:8 but the fearful and unbelieving, the abominable, and murderers, and whoremongers, and sorcerers, and idolaters, and all liars, shall have their part in the Lake which burns with fire and brimstone: which is the second death

John 13:13 and no man has descended up to heaven but he that came down from heaven even the Son of man which is in heaven

1 Corinthians 15:51 behold I show you a

mystery we shall not all sleep but we shall all be changed

1 Corinthians 15:52 in a moment in the twinkling of an eye, at the last Trump: for the trumpet shall sound and the dead shall be raised incorruptible and we shall be changed

2 Thessalonians 2:9 Behold I come quickly and my reward is with me

Ephesians 6:8 knowing that whatsoever good thing any man does, the same shall he receive of the Lord, whether he be bond or free

Hebrews 9:27 It is appointed unto men once to die, after that the judgment

OF NOTE; …..won't prevent those, which are asleep.

The saints, which died in Christ, will he return with them to meet him in the air. He will judge the 'quick and the dead,'

Hebrews 6:2 of the doctrine of baptisms, and of laying on of hands, and of the resurrection of the dead, and of eternal judgment

2 Corinthians 12:2 I knew a man in Christ above fourteen years ago, (whether in the body, I cannot tell; or whether out of the body, I cannot tell: God knows;) such as one caught up to the third heaven

2 Corinthians 12:3 and I knew such a man (whether in the body, or out of the body, I cannot tell: God knows)

2 Corinthians 12:4 How that he was caught up into paradise, and heard unspeakable words, which is not lawful for a man to utter

2 Corinthians 12:5 of such as one will, will I glory: yet of myself will not glory, but in mine affirmities

Acts 10:42 he commanded us to preach to the people, and testify that is he which was ordained of God to be the judge of the quick and the dead

1 Peter 4:5 who shall give account to him to judge the quick and the dead

A Case In Point: 'the dead in Christ,' are described in this verse, 'of which are asleep, 'when Christ returns

1 Thessalonians 4:17 then we which are alive and remain shall be caught up together with them in the clouds to meet the Lord in the air; and so shall we ever be with the Lord

OF NOTE: "caught up," is not a word origin for "rapture." And neither is, "catching up,"

A Case In Point: the 'alive and remain,' will be like those which are 'asleep,' in Jesus, to meet God in the air.

OF NOTE; "meet," is not 'join,' it did not say, "return," with Christ. You cannot ascend into God's kingdom with Jesus Christ. The 'air,' is not God's kingdom. The air is a firmament of heaven. In fact, the verse never said, "heaven."

2 Thessalonians 2:9 Behold I come quickly an my reward is with me

OF NOTE; my 'reward,' are the saints in the first resurrection, or, those that are 'asleep."

Ezra 7:10 for Ezra has prepared his heart to seek the law of the Lord, and to do it, and to teach Israel statues and judgments

OF NOTE; prepare your hearts to meet God, as Ezra did.

Revelation 3:2 Be watchful and strengthen the things which remain that are ready to die: for I have not found thy works perfect before God

1 Thessalonians 4:18 wherefore comfort one another with these words

Matthew 16:28 Verily I say unto you, There be some standing here, which shall not taste of death, till they see the Son of man coming in his kingdom

you won't be able to see God in the flesh

Daniel 12:2 And many of them that sleep in the dust of the earth shall awake, some to everlasting life, some to shame and everlasting contempt.

A Case In Point: the saints that sleep in the dust, to everlasting life, are in the first resurrection, and the latter in the second resurrection, which is the second death.

Chapter Eight
Jesus Ascends into Heaven

For this Chapter, it should be made noted, that the ascension of Jesus Christ is vastly different, as the departure of prophets, and of the apostles.

Mark 16:19 So then after the Lord had spoken unto them, he was received up into heaven, and sat on the right hand of God

OF NOTE: Enoch, nor Elijah, or any other prophet, or apostle, such as Philip or John, were 'received,' up into heaven

Acts 1:9 and when he had spoken these things, while they beheld, he was taken up; and a cloud received him out of sight

Acts 1:11 which also said ye men of Galilee, why stand up gazing up into heaven? This same Jesus, which is taken up from you into heaven, shall, so come in like manner, as ye have seen him go into heaven.

OF NOTE; the men of Galilee stood gazing into heaven, because they did not witness Jesus coming down to earth, as did, the sons of the prophets, when Elijah went up to heaven. They went searching for Elijah on the ground, in the mountains, and in the valley. No such search was ever made for Jesus Christ, when he ascended into his Father's kingdom.

A Case In Point: Elijah 'went up', instead of 'taken up.' No one received Elijah into God's kingdom, at that point, and time. Whereas, Jesus was received into heaven, when he ascended.

OF NOTE; The two witnesses of Revelation were not hidden by clouds, 'out of sight,' as was Jesus Christ.

Acts 1:3 while he showed himself alive after his passion of many infallible beliefs.

A Case In Point: Jesus was alive, when he ascended into heaven. Elijah, on the other hand, went up to heaven. Elijah later died, and went to heaven, not taken up to heaven of heavens, in a whirlwind

Luke 24:34 Saying, The Lord is risen indeed, and has appeared to Simon

Acts 2:34 for David is not ascended into heaven. 1 Kings 2:1, and 2:10

John 3:13 no man ascended into heaven, but that come down from heaven, even the Son of man which is in heaven

John 8:23 ye are from beneath; I am from above: ye are of this world; I am not of this world

A Case In Point: Jesus Christ was alive before he ascended into heaven. David, also, was not from heaven, so, he could not return through ascension.

Acts 2:34 for David is not ascended into the heavens: but he said himself, The Lord said unto my lord, Sit thou on my right hand

Acts 2:35 Until I make thy foes thy footstool

Romans warns us not to be in doubt or to be suggestive about whom ascends into heaven, in the first place.

Romans 10:6 but the righteous which is of faith speaks on the wise, Say not in thine heart, who shall ascend into heaven? (that is, to bring Christ down from above)

Romans 10:7 Or, who shall descend from the deep? (that is, to bring up Christ again from the dead

John 1:51 verily, verily, I say unto you, Hereafter you shall see heaven open, and the angels of God ascending and descending upon the Son of man

John 3:13 and no man ascended up to heaven, but he that came down from heaven, even the Son of man which is in heaven

John 5:37 And the Father himself, which has sent me, hath borne witness of me. Ye have neither heard his voice at any time, nor seen his shape.

John 6:46 not that any man has seen the Father, save which he is of God, he has seen the Father

1 John 4:12 No man has seen God at any time....

Exodus 33:20 and he said, Thou cannot see my

face; for there can no man see my face and Live

John 8:21 I go my way and he shall seek me, and shall die in your sins; whither I go you cannot come

John 20:18 Mary Magdalene told Jesus' disciples, she had seen the Lord.

John 20:20 Jesus appears to his disciples

John 20:25 we have seen the Lord

John 20:17 Touch me not: For I am not yet ascended to my Father: but go to my brethren, and say unto them, I ascend unto my Father, to my God, and to your God.

John 21:23 then went this saying; abroad among the brethren, that that disciple should not die: yet Jesus said unto him, he shall not die: but, if I will tarry come, what is that to thee?

OF NOTE: The disciple should not die a second death. He cannot avoid the first resurrection, but he can the second one.

John 16:28 I come forth from the Father, and am come into the world: again, I leave the world and go to my Father.

A Case In Point: Enoch, and Elijah, king David, Mary, the mother of Jesus, Melchisedec, Philip, the two witnesses, Abraham, Isaac, and Jacob, or Moses, Daniel, John the Baptist, Jeremiah, Paul, etc, were not gods, and therefore did not ascend into heaven, where God's kingdom is. These aforementioned individuals, not only were they not gods, or goddesses, but because they were not from heaven, as was, Jesus Christ.

Noah, Lot, Job, perfect individuals, and yet did not ascend into heaven. God helped Lot escape to a mountain. Noah, was told to build an ark. Job recovered from his boils.

2 Thessalonians 2:9 Behold I come quickly and my reward is with me

Acts 10:25 And as Peter was coming in, Cornelius met him, and fell down at his feet

Acts 10:26 But Peter took him up, Saying, Stand up; I myself also am a man

Acts 14:15 ……. We are men also of like passions with you……..

Acts 28:6 howbeit they looked when he should have swollen, or fallen down dead suddenly: but after they had looked a great while and saw no harm come to him, they changed their minds, and said he was a god.

1 Timothy 3:16 and without controversy great is the mystery of Godliness: God was manifest in the flesh, justified in the Spirit, seen of angels, preached unto the Gentiles, believed on in the world, received up into glory

Luke 10:19 I give you power to tread down serpents and scorpions.

John 6:62 what and if you shall see the Son of man ascend up where he was before?

John 6:63 It is the spirit that quickens: the flesh profits nothing: ......

Luke 24:23 and when they found not his body, they came, saying, that they had also seen a vision of angels, which said that he was alive.

Luke 24:34 Saying, the Lord is risen indeed, and has appeared to Simon

Luke 24:36 and as they thus spoke, Jesus himself stood in the midst of them, and said unto them, Peace be unto you

John 21:14 This is now the third time that Jesus showed himself to his disciples, after that he was risen from the dead

Luke 24:24 and certain of them which were with us went to the sepulchre, and found it even so as the women had said: but him they saw not

Luke 24:51 it came to pass while he blessed them, he was parted from them, and carried up into heaven.

OF NOTE; Jesus carried up, by angels of the Lord. The angels were also from heaven, John 3:13...except he came from heaven

OF NOTE; as Jesus was carried into the kingdom of God, he was separated from his disciples, they were "left behind." The disciples were Christians. Just because you are left behind, doesn't mean, you are among the unsaved.

2 Corinthians 12:4 now that he was caught into

Paradise.

OF NOTE; Paradise is the heaven of heavens, where God is. Jesus Christ, therefore, is the only one to ascend directly into heaven, where his Father is.

Ephesians 4:9 (now that he ascended, what is it but he also first ascended first into the lower parts of the earth?

Ephesians 4:10 he that descended is the same also that ascended up far above all heavens, that he might fill all things.)

A Case In Point: Jesus ascended far 'above all heavens,' whereas, Elijah, and the two witnesses, didn't make it that far. They only reached firmament of heaven, as described in Genesis 1:6-8.

John 19:26 Jesus saw his mother Woman behold thy son

Daniel 7:13 I saw in the night visions, and, behold, one like the Son of man came with the clouds of heaven, and came to the ancient of days, and they brought him near before him.

Revelation 12:5 And she brought forth a man child, who was to rule all nations with a rod of iron: her child was caught up unto God and to his throne

Revelation 12:6 And the woman fled into the wilderness where she has a place prepared of God, that they should feed her there a thousand two hundred and threescore days

Exodus 33:20 and he said, Thou cannot see my

face; for there can no man see my face and live.

Chapter Nine
Jesus' Teachings

Jesus' taught love, righteousness, repentance, separation, translation, transformed, changed, sufferings, kingdom of God, forgiveness,

watch, pray, escape, Since Jesus never taught of a 'rapture," instead, he tried to dissuade such talk to his apostles.

Matthew 13:25 and the stars of heaven shall fall, and powers that are in heaven shall be shaken

Matthew 13:26 and then shall they see the Son of man, coming in clouds with great power and glory

Matthew 13:32 and that day and hour knows no man, no, not the angels which are in heaven, neither the son, but the Father

Matthew 13:33 Take heed, watch and pray: For ye know not when the time is

Matthew 13:37 he that sows good seed is the Son of man

Matthew 13:38 the field is the world; the good seed are the children of the kingdom; but the tares are the children of the wicked one

Matthew 13:39 the enemy that sowed them is the devil; the harvest is the end of the world; and the reapers are the angels

Matthew 13:40 as therefore the tares are gathered and burned in the fire; so shall it be at the end of the world

Matthew 13:41 Son of man shall send for his angels they shall gather out of his kingdom all them that offend, and them which do iniquity

Matthew 13:42 and shall cast them into furnace of fire; there shall be weeping and gnashing of teeth

Matthew 13:49 so shall it be at the end of the world: the angels shall come forth and sever the wicked from among the just

Matthew 13:50 and cast them into furnace of fire; there shall be weeping and gnashing of teeth

Matthew 22:11 when the king came in to see the guests, he saw there a man which had not on a wedding garment

Matthew 22:13 then said the king to the servants Bind him hand and foot, and take him away, and cast him into outer darkness; there shall be weeping and gnashing of teeth

Matthew 25:30 and cast the unprofitable servant into outer darkness; there shall be weeping and gnashing of teeth

Matthew 16:28 verily I say unto you, there be some standing here, which shall not taste of death, until they see the Son of man coming in his kingdom.

'until' means, they will eventually see death

Matthew 25:32 and before them shall be gathered all nations: and he shall separate them one from another, as a shepherd divides his sheep from goats

Matthew 25:33 he shall set the sheep on his right hand and the goats on the left

Matthew 26:41 watch and pray that ye enter not into temptation

1 Thessalonians 5:2 for yourselves know perfectly that the day of the Lord comes as a thief in the night

1 Thessalonians 5:3 For when they shall say, Peace and Safety; then sudden destruction comes upon them, as travail upon a woman with child; and they shall not escape

Revelation 5:4 But ye, brethren, are not in darkness, that day should overtake you as a thief.

A Case In Point: Revelation 3:2 Be watchful, and strengthen the things which remain, that are ready to die: for I have not found thy works perfect before God

Revelation 3:3 Remember how therefore how thou has received and heard and hold fast, and repent. If therefore thou shall not watch, I will come on thee as a thief, and thou shall not know what hour I will come upon thee

2 Corinthians 5:17 therefore if anyone is in

Christ, he is a new creature, the old things passed away, behold, new things have come

Colossians 1:13 giving thanks to the power of darkness, and has translated us into the kingdom of his dear son.

Hebrews 11:5 by faith Enoch was translated that he should not see death; and was not found because God translated him: for before his translation he had his testimony that he pleased God.

1 Peter 1:22 seeing you have purified your souls in obeying the truth through the Spirit into unfeigned love of the brethren, see that ye love one another with a pure heart fervently:

1 Peter 1:23 being born again not of corruptible seed, but of incorruptible, by the word of God, which lives and abides forever.

John 7:34 you shall seek me and shall not find me: and where I am thither you cannot come.

John 11:25 I am the resurrection and the life: he that believes in me, though he were dead, yet shall he live

John 11:26 and whosoever lives and believes in me shall never die. Believes thou this?

John 21:22 if I will that he tarry till I come, what is that to thee? follow thou me.

John 21:23 this went this saying abroad among the brethren, that that disciple should not die: yet Jesus said not unto him, he shall not die: but, If I will he tarry till I come, what is that to thee?

OF NOTE; Jesus meant, this disciple, that Peter saw, cannot ascend into heaven with Jesus. Jesus said the disciple will die, however, the first resurrection, and but, not die, the second death, which is the second resurrection.

OF NOTE; that disciple in this verse, won't die the second death, and raised in the second resurrection, which has no power

Luke 9:27 then came to him certain of the Sadducees, which deny there is any resurrection; and they asked him

Revelation 20:6 …. on such the second death

Hebrews 9:27 it is appointed unto man once to die, after that the judgment

OF NOTE; no ascension into the sky, or heaven, with Jesus Christ, alive or dead.

John 16:10 of righteousness I go to my

Father and ye see me no more

John 13:33 Little children, yet a little while, I am with you. You shall seek me; and as I said unto the Jews, Whither I go you cannot come; so now I say unto you

John 13:36 Whiter I go thou cannot follow me, Jesus said to Simon Peter, thou cannot follow me now; but thou shall follow me afterwards

John 13:37 Peter said unto him Lord, why cannot I follow you now? I will lay down my life for thy sake

John 13:38 Jesus answered: will thou lay down your life for my sake? Verily, verily I say unto thee, The cock shall crow, till thou has deceived me thrice.

OF NOTE; don't justify yourself to think, you should be ascended up with Jesus Christ. Luke 14:11 for whosoever exalts himself shall be abased; and he that humbles himself shall be exalted

Luke 9:27 but I tell you of a truth, there be some standing here, which shall not taste death, till they see the kingdom of God

Luke 13:35 Believe it not when they say there is Christ

Luke 21:3 but take heed to yourselves lest you be overcharged with surfeiting, and drunkenness, and cares of this life, and so that day come upon you unawares

Luke 21:33 Heaven and earth shall not pass away: but words shall not pass away

Luke 21:34 take heed to yourselves lest anytime your heart be overcharged with surfeiting, and drunkenness and cares of this life, and so that day come upon you unawares

Luke 21:35 for a snare shall come upon all of them on the face of them that dwell upon the whole earth

Luke 21:36 Watch ye therefore and pray to

escape all these things that shall come to pass, and to stand before the Son of man

Luke 23:34 Father forgive them for they know not what they do.

2 Peter 3:10 the day of the Lord will come as a thief in the night…….

2 Peter 3:14 Wherefore, beloved, seeing that ye look for such things, be diligent that ye may be found of him in peace

2 Timothy 2:12 if we suffer we will also reign with him

Hebrews 2:9 we see Jesus who was made a little lower than the angels for the suffering of death. 2:10 …bring many sons to glory to make the captain of their salvation perfect through sufferings

Hebrews 9:27 it is appointed unto men once to die, after this the judgment

1 Peter 1:11 Searching what. Or what manner of time the Spirit of Christ which was in them did signify, when it testified before hand the sufferings of Christ, and the glory that should follow

1 Peter 3:17 it is better if the will of God be so that ye suffer for well doing than for evil doing

Revelation 2:10 Fear none of those things which thou shall suffer: ……

Revelation 3:3 Remember therefore how thou has received and heard and hold fast, repent. If therefore, thou shall not watch, I will come on thee as a thief, and thou shall not know what hour I will come upon thee

Revelation 3:10 Because thou has kept the world of my patience, I will also keep thee from the hour of temptation, which shall come upon all of the world, to try them that dwell upon the earth

1 Corinthians 10:13 there has no temptation taken you but such as is common to man: but God is faithful, who will not suffer you to be tempted above all that ye are able; but will with the temptation also make a way to escape, that ye may be able to bear it

Mark 13:13 but ye shall be hated of all men for my name's sake: but he that endure till the end the same shall be saved

Matthew 6:13 and lead us not into temptation but deliver us from evil: for thine is the kingdom, and the power, and the glory, forever, Amen

John 14:6 I am the way, the truth, and the light, no man comes unto the Father, but by me

John 10:9 I am the door: by me if any man enter in he shall be saved, and shall go in and out, and find pasture

OF NOTE; no man comes unto the Father, but by me.

'by me,' not 'with me.' He didn't say, ascend with him to see the Father, but rather, by me.

John 1:18 No man has seen God at any time; the

only begotten Son, which is in the bosom of the Father, he has declared him

John 14:19 yet a little while and the world shall see me no more

John 19:26 Jesus saw his mother Woman behold your son

John 8:21 I go my way, and ye shall seek me, and shall die in your sins; wither I go ye cannot come

John 8:24 …if ye believe I am not the he, ye shall die in your sins

John 7:34 ye shall seek me and shall not find me. And where I am thither you cannot come

John 21:23 then went this saying, abroad among the brethren, that that disciple should not die; yet Jesus said unto him, he shall not die; but, if I will he tarry till I come, what is that to thee?

2 Corinthians 5:17 therefore if anyone is in Christ, he is a new creature; the old things passed away; behold, old things are passed away

Matthew 24:5 for many shall come in my name and shall deceive many

OF NOTE: Yeshua, is a false Christ, and Yahwe is a false god. Both are idols. Yeshua is not the messiah

Matthew 24:9 then shall they deliver you up to be afflicted, and they shall kill you: and ye shall be hated of all nations for my name's sake

Revelation 12:7 and there was war in heaven:

Michael and his angels fought against the dragon, and the dragon fought and his angels

Matthew 24:24 For false messiahs and false prophets will appear and perform great signs and wonders to deceive, if possible the very elect

2 Corinthians 11:13 for such as false prophets, deceitful workers, transforming themselves into apostles of light

OF NOTE: not all transforming is good

Romans 12:2 be ye not transformed to this world: but be ye transformed by the renewing of your mind, that ye may prove what is that good and acceptable, and perfect, will of God

2 Corinthians 11:14 and no marvel; for Satan himself is transformed into a angel of light

OF NOTE; This disciple wanted to return into heaven with Jesus Christ, But he could not. Instead, Jesus told him to tarry till he comes again. The disciple also will have to die, and be in the first resurrection, but, he could avoid the second death. Yeshua is a false messiah

Matthew 24:24, Yahwe, is a false god,
Psalms 83:18

Chapter Ten
Jesus Suffered Tribulation

2 Timothy 3:12 yea and all that love godly in Christ Jesus shall suffer persecution

A Case In Point: Evangelicals, Jews, Catholics will suffer with the unsaved in the great tribulation

2 Timothy 2:12 if we suffer with him, we shall also reign with him…

Philippians 1:29 for unto you it is given in the behalf of Christ, not only to believe on him, but also to suffer for his sake

Hebrew 2:9 we see Jesus who was made a little lower than the angels for the suffering of death

Philippians 2:10 …bring man sons to glory to make the captain of their salvation perfect through suffering

1 Peter 1:11 searching what, or what manner of time the Spirit of Christ which was in them did signify, which testified before hand the sufferings of Christ, and the glory that should follow

1 Peter 3:17 it is better if the will of God be so that ye suffer for well doing than for evil doing

1 Peter 3:18 for Jesus Christ also once suffered for sins the just for the unjust to bring us to God

Luke 18:32 for he shall be delivered to the Gentiles and shall be mocked and spitefully behehaed and spitted on

Luke 18:33 and they shall scourge him, and put him to death: and the third day he shall rise again

John 24:26 ought not Christ to have suffered these things, and to enter into his glory?

Mark 110:33-34 Behold we go to Jerusalem; and the Son of man shall be delivered unto the chief priests, and unto scribes; and they shall condemn, and shall deliver him to the Gentiles

Mark 10:34 and they shall mock him and shall scourge him, and shall spit on him, and shall kill him; and the third day he shall rise again

Luke 24:26 it behoved Christ to suffer, and to rise from the dead the third day

1 Peter 2:9 Christ suffered for us

1 Peter 2:22 who did no sin neither guile found in his mouth

Hebrews 2:18 for that he himself has suffered being tempted, he is able to succor them that are tempted.

Matthew 17:23 but I say unto you Elijah is come already, and they knew him not, but did unto him, whatsoever they would. So shall the Son of man also suffer of them

Chapter Eleven
The Great Tribulation

Jeremiah 30:7 Alas! For that day is great so that none is like it, it is even the time of Jacob's trouble, but he shall be saved out of it

Romans 2:9 Tribulation and anguish, upon every soul of man that does evil, of the Jew first, and also of the Gentile

Matthew 24:21 For there shall be great tribulation such as was not since the beginning of the world to this time, no, nor ever shall be

Matthew 24:29 immediately after the tribulation in those days shall the sun be darkened, and the moon shall not give her light, and the stars shall fall from heaven, and the powers of the heavens shall be shaken

Matthew 24:30 and then shall appear the sign of the Son of man in heaven: and then shall all the tribes of the earth mourn, and they shall see the Son of man coming in the clouds of heaven with power and great glory

John 16:33 these things have I spoken unto you, that in me you might have peace. In the world you shall have tribulation: but be of good cheer: I have overcome the world.

Revelation 6:17 for the great day of wrath is come; and who shall be able to stand?

Revelation 2:22 Behold I will cast her into a bed, and them that commit adultery with her into great tribulation, except they repent of their deeds

Luke 3:7 O generation of vipers, who has warned you to flee from the wrath to come?

Luke 21:35 for a share is come upon them that dwell upon all of the earth

Acts 14:22 …we must through much tribulation enter into the kingdom of God

2 Timothy 2:12 if we suffer we shall also reign with him

2 Timothy 3:12 yea and all that live godly in Christ Jesus shall suffer persecution

Philippians 1:29 for unto you it is given in the behalf of Christ, not only to believe on him, but also to suffer for his sake

Revelation 7:13 And one of the elders answered, saying unto me, What are these which are arrayed in white robes? And whence came they?

Revelation 7:14 And I said unto him, Sir, thou knows And he said unto me, These are they which came out the great tribulation, and have washed their robes and, and made them white in the blood of the Lamb.

A Case In Point: These are the saints, and not the

"left behind," or the "unsaved," in the second resurrection.

A Case In Point: Revelation 18:24 and in her was found the blood of the prophets, and of saints, and all that was slain upon the earth

Deuteronomy 4:30 when thou are in tribulation, and all these things are come upon thee, even in the latter days, if thou turn to the Lord thy God, and be obedient to his voice;

Deuteronomy 4:31 (For the Lord thy God is a merciful God;) he will not forsake thee, neither destroy thee, nor forget the covenant of thy fathers which he sware unto them,

Jeremiah 30:7 Alas! For that day is great that so that none is like it; it is even the time of Jacob's trouble; but he shall be saved out of it

Isaiah 13:6 Howl ye, for the day of the Lord is at hand, it shall come as a destruction from the Almighty

Isaiah 13:9 Behold, the day of the Lord comes, cruel both with wrath and fierce anger, to lay the land desolate: and he shall destroy the sinners thereof out of it

Jeremiah 30:7 Alas! For that day is great so that none is like it: it is even the time of Jacob's trouble; but he shall be saved out of it

Daniel 12:1 And at that time shall Michael stand up, the great prince which stands for the children of thy people: and there shall be a time of trouble, such as never was since there was a nation even to the same time: and at that time thy people shall be delivered, every one that shall be found written in the book.

Daniel 12:2 And many of them that sleep in the dust of the earth shall awake, some to everlasting life, some to shame and everlasting contempt

Zephaniah 1:15 That day is a day of wrath, a day of trouble and distress, a day of wasteness, and desolation, and darkness and gloominess, a day of clouds and thick darkness

Zephaniah 1:16 A day of the Trumpet and alarm against the fenced cities, and against the high towers

Zephaniah 1:17 And I will bring distress among men, that they should walk like blind men, because they have sinned against the Lord: and their blood shall be poured out as dust, and their flesh as the dung

Zephaniah 1:18 Neither their silver and their gold shall be able to deliver them in the day of the Lord's wrath, but the whole land shall be devoured by the fire of his jealousy; for he shall make even a speedy riddance of all them that dwell in the land

2 Corinthians 7:4 Great is my boldness of speech toward you, great is my glorying of you: I am filled with comfort, I am exceeding joyful in all our

tribulation

Philippians 1:29 for unto you it is given on the behalf of Christ, not only to believe on him, but also to suffer for his sake

2 Corinthians 7:4 I am filled with comfort. I am exceedingly joyful in all tribulation

Revelation 3:10 because thou has kept the word of my patience, I will also keep thee from the hour of temptation, which shall come upon all the world, to try them that dwell upon the earth

Revelation 20:4 I saw them beheaded for the witness of Jesus, and for the word of God, which had not worshipped the beast and his image, or in their hands, reigned with Christ for a thousand years

Revelation 22:12 Behold I come quickly and my reward is with me to give unto every man according to his work shall be

Daniel 7:27 the kingdom and dominion, and the greatness of the kingdom under the whole heaven, shall be given to the people of the saints of the most High, Whose kingdom is an everlasting kingdom, and all dominions shall serve and obey him

Revelation 9:6 and in those days shall men seek death, and shall not find it; and shall desire to die, and death shall flee from them

Chapter Twelve
The Saints and the Great Tribulation

Romans 1:7 to all that be in Rome, beloved of God, called to be saints: Grace to you and peace from God our Father, and the Lord Jesus Christ

The Saints will be in the great tribulation, and not, "caught up, "somewhere, into the heavens, safe and free, from the troubles, they helped create in the first place. Many preachers, theologians, priests, teachers, are in awe, confused, troubled, in doubt, and in disbelief, at the bible scriptures, to even warn their congregations, what is about to take place, in the end times.

Saints cannot ascend into heaven, with Jesus Christ, in the same spiritual way, as Jesus Christ did, because saints are also sinners. In fact, the saints, will more than likely, propel the coming antichrist, the son of perdition, the beast, or that wicked one, into position of world power one day, if they haven't done so already.

The antichrist will accomplish this through, none other, than deception. And to conqueror their fears, they come up with the false hope of a "rapture." Saints are in for a rude awakening, if they believe, God will reward them for their actions.

Revelation 2:4 Nevertheless I have somewhat against thee, because thou left thy first love

Psalms 37:28 for the Lord loves judgment and forsakes not his saints; they are preserved forever

Psalms 51:5 gather my saints together unto me those that made a covenant with me for sacrifice

Psalms 79:2 the dead bodies of the servants have they given to be meat unto fowls of the heaven, flesh of saints unto beasts of the earth

Psalms 79:3 the blood have they shed like water round about Jerusalem; there was none to bury them

Psalms 116:15 precious in the sight of the Lord is death of his saints

Revelation 3:2 I have not found your works perfect before God

Revelation 12:17 And the dragon was wroth with the woman and went to make war with the remnant of her seed, which keep the commandments of God, and have the testimony of Jesus Christ

1 Corinthians 10:32 Give none offence, neither the Jews, nor then to the Jews, nor to the Gentiles, nor to the Church of God

2 Peter 2:4 For God spared not the angels that sinned, but cast them down to hell, and delivered them to chains of darkness to be reserved unto

judgment

Job 4:18 he puts no trust even in his servants: and against his angels: He charges error

Job 15:15 behold he puts no trust in his saints, the heavens are not clean in his sight

Job 25:5 Behold even the moon, and it shines not; yea, even the stars are not pure in his sight

A Case In Point: 'the remnant of her seed, 'are the saints.

Revelation 13:17 And that no man might buy or sell, save he that had the mark, or the name of the beast, or the number of his name

Daniel 7:18 the saints of the most High shall take the kingdom, and possess the kingdom forever, and ever and ever

Daniel 7:21 I beheld, the same horn made war with the saints

Daniel 7:22 until the ancient days came, and judgment was given to the saints of the most High; and the time came the saints possessed the kingdom

Daniel 7:25 he shall speak great words against the most High, and shall wear out the saints of the most high, and think to change times and laws: and they shall be given into his hand until a time and times dividing the time

Daniel 7:26 but the judgment shall sit, and they shall take away his dominion, to consume and to destroy it unto the end.

Daniel 7:27 And the Kingdom and Dominion, and the greatness of the kingdom under the whole heaven, shall be given to the people of the saints of the most High, whose kingdom is an everlasting kingdom, and all dominions shall serve and obey him

Daniel 8:13 I heard one saint speaking, and another saint said unto that certain saint spoke, How long shall the vision concerning the daily sacrifice, and the transgression of daily sacrifice, and transgression of desolation, to give both the sanctuary and the host to be trodden under foot

Romans 3:23 all have sinned and come short of the glory of God.

Romans 5:2 wherefore by one man entered into the world and death by sin and so death passed upon all men: for that all have sinned.

Romans 5:12 Wherefore, as by one man sin entered into the world, and death by sin; and so death passed upon all men, for they all have sinned.

1 John 1:8 you say we have no sin we deceive ourselves

1 John 1:10 you say we have not sinned we make him a liar and his word is not in us

1 John 3:5 ye know that he was manifested to take away our sins, and in him is no sin.

John 16:33 in the world you shall have

tribulation……..

Acts 14:22 …we must through much tribulation enter into kingdom of God

2 Timothy 2:12 if we suffer we shall also reign with him

2 Timothy 3:12 yea and all that live godly by Christ Jesus shall suffer persecution

Philippians 1:21 For to me is live in Christ, and to die is gain

Philippians 1:29 for unto you it is given in the behalf of Christ, not only to believe on him, but also to suffer for his sake

A Case In Point: since saints are sinners, they will die the death; for they have sinned at some point and time. Which is why saints cannot ascend directly into heaven.

Romans 3:23 for we all have sinned and come short of the glory of God

Romans 3:10 as it is written, there is not righteous no, not, one

Revelation 7:13 and one of the elders answered, saying unto me, What are these which are arrayed in white robes? and whence came they?

Revelation 7:14 and I said unto him, Sir, thou knows, and he said to me, These are they which came out of the great tribulation, and have washed their robes, and made them white in the blood of the Lamb.

A Case In Point: Christians, saints, evangelicals, Protestants, Catholics, Jews, and any other kindred, will be turned over to the antichrist, to overcome them, and kill them.

Romans 2:9 Tribulation and anguish upon every soul of man that does evil, of the Jew first, and also of the Gentile

Because to die is to gain. Philippians 1:21 for to me is live in Christ, and to die is gain

Job 16:11 God has turned me over to the ungodly, and turned me over to the hands of the wicked.

Job 3:26 I was not in safety neither had I rest, neither was I quiet; yet trouble came

Revelation 20:4 I saw the souls of them beheaded for the witness of Jesus and for the word of God which had not worshipped the beast neither his image neither had receive his mark upon their foreheads, or in their hands; and they lived and reigned with Christ a thousand years.

A Case In point: This scripture is not addressing "those left behind." This scripture is about the saints.

The non-Christians, are the individuals, many believe, are "left behind," and have already taken the mark of the beast, in their foreheads, or hands, and worshipped the beast and his image.

The saints, or Christians, that are in the great

tribulation will be beheaded. However these saints did not take the mark of the beast in their foreheads, or in their hands, or worshipped the beast and his image.

The Beast makes war with the saints, to overcome them, and kill them. Daniel 7:21 This verse is about the first resurrection, as well.

OF NOTE; These saints that are in tribulation, and are about to be beheaded, most likely, made the mistake of voting the antichrist into world prominence and power.

'These saints will quickly realize they made a mistake, after they cast their vote. But it will be too late to reject the mark of the beast. There has been speculation, that 60%, to as high as 81%, of evangelicals voted en-masse, for the nation's forty-fifth President.

Ephesians 5:6 Let no man deceive you with vain words: for because of these things come the word of God upon the children of disobedience

2 Thessalonians 2:11 and for this cause God shall send strong delusion that they should believe a lie

Revelation 16:6 For they have shed the blood of saints, and prophets, and thou has given them blood to drink; for they are worthy

Isaiah 24:17 Fear, and the pit, and the snare, are upon thee, O inhabitant of the earth.

1 Peter 4:12 Behold, think it not strange

concerning the fiery trial which is to try you, as though some strange thing happened to you

Revelation 3:10 Because thou has kept the word of my patience, I will also keep thee from the hour of temptation, which shall come upon all of the world, to try them that dwell upon the earth

Revelation 6:9 And when he had opened the fifth seal, I saw under the altar the souls of them that were slain for the word of God, and for the testimony which they held

Revelation 7:14 And I said unto him, Sir. Thou knows. And he said unto me, These are they which came out of the great tribulation, and have washed their robes and made them white in the blood of the Lamb.

Revelation 7:15 Therefore are they before the throne of God, and serve him day and night in his temple: and he that sits on the throne shall dwell among them

Revelation 7:16 They shall hunger no more, neither thirst anymore; neither shall the sun light on them, nor any heat.

Revelation 7:17 For the Lamb in the midst of the throne shall feed them, and lead them unto living fountains of waters; and God shall wipe away all tears from their eyes

Revelation 8:13 And I beheld, and heard an angel flying through the midst of heaven, saying with a loud voice, Woe, woe, woe, to the inhabitants of the earth by reason of the other voices of the trumpet of the three angels, which are yet to sound!

Revelation 8:3 and another angel came and stood at the altar, having a golden censer: and there was given unto him much incense; that he should offer it with prayers of all saints upon the golden altar which was before the throne

Revelation 9:4 …. but only those men which had not the seal of God in their foreheads.

OF NOTE: the saints are still here in this verse. The locusts are commanded to inflict pain on the wicked.

Revelation 11:7 And when they shall have finished their testimony, the beast that ascends out of the bottomless pit shall make war against them, and shall overcome them, and kill them

Revelation 13:7 it was given to him to make war with the saints, and to overcome them: and power was given him over all kindred, and tongues, and nations

Revelation 13:8 and all that dwell upon the earth shall worship him, whose names are not written in the book of life of the Lamb slain from the foundation of the world

Revelation 14:1 And, I looked, and, Lo, a

Lamb stood on the mount Sion, and with him a hundred and forty four thousand, having his

Father's name written in their foreheads

Revelation 14:3 And they sung as it were a new song before the throne, and before the four beasts, and the elders; and no man could learn that song but the hundred and forty four thousand

Revelation 14:4 These are they which were defiled with women; for they are virgins. These are they which follow the Lamb

withers ever he goes. These were redeemed from among men, being the first fruits unto God and to the Lamb

Revelation 15:2 And I saw as it were a sea of glass mingled with fire; and them that had gotten the victory over the beast, and over his image, and over his mark, and over the number of his name, stand on the sea of glass, having the harps of God

Revelation 15:3 And they sing the song of Moses the servant of God, and the song of the Lamb, saying, Great and marvelous are thy works, Lord God Almighty; Just and true are thy ways, thou King of saints

Revelation 17:8 I saw the woman drunken with blood of the saints, and with the blood of the martyrs of Jesus

Revelation 17:14 these shall make war with the Lamb, and the Lamb shall overcome them: for he is Lord of lords, and King of kings: and they that are with him are called, chosen and faithful

Revelation 18:24 And in her was found the blood of the prophets, and of saints, and of all that were slain upon the earth.

Revelation 19:1 AND after those things I heard a great voice of much people in heaven, saying, Alleluia; Salvation and glory, and honor, and power, unto the Lord our God

Revelation 20:4 I saw thrones, and they sat upon them, and judgment was given unto them: and I saw the souls of them that were beheaded for the witness of Jesus, and for the word of God, which had not worshipped the beast, and neither his image, neither had received his mark upon their foreheads, or in their hands; and they lived and reigned with Christ a thousand years

OF NOTE; even if the saints made mistakes by voting the antichrist into the seat of world power, the only way out for them, is to reject the beast's image, number, and mark, and they can still go to heaven.

Acts 28:28 be it known therefore unto you, that the salvation of God is sent unto the Gentiles, and that they will hear it

Matthew 3:7 But when he saw many of the

Pharisees and Sadducees come to his baptism, he said unto them, O generation of vipers, who has warned you to flee from the wrath to come!

Matthew 12:34 O generation of vipers, how can

ye, being evil speak good things, for out of the abundance of the heart the mouth speaks

Matthew 21:43 Therefore I say unto you the kingdom of God shall be taken from you and given to a nation bringing forth the fruits thereof

Luke 3:7 And said to the multitude that came forth to be baptized of him, O generation of vipers, who has warned you to flee from the wrath to come?

Luke 3:8 Bring forth therefore fruits worthy of repentance, and began not to say within yourselves, We have Abraham our father: for I say unto you, That God is able of these stones to raise up children unto Abraham

Romans 9:25 I will call them my people which are not my people; and her beloved which are not beloved

Romans 9:27 Esaias cried, concerning Israel, Though the number of the children of Israel be as the sand of the sea, a remnant shall be saved

Romans 11:11 I say then, Have they stumbled that they should fall? God forbid: but rather through their fall salvation is come upon the Gentiles, for to provoke them to jealousy

OF NOTE; Not all Israel is Israel

OF NOTE; if any one disputes, whether, or not, anyone is in heaven, this should underscore this.

OF NOTE; Saints are in for rude awakening, if

they believe they won't be in the great tribulation.

Revelation 20:4 And I saw thrones, and they sat upon them, and judgment was given unto them: and I saw the souls of them that were beheaded for the witness of Jesus, and for the word of God, which had no worshipped the beast, neither his image, neither had received his mark upon their foreheads, or in their hands; and they lived, and reigned with Christ a thousand years.

OF NOTE; These are not the non-Christians, because the non-Christians, had already worshipped the beast, and his image, and received the mark on their foreheads, and hands.

These non-Christians aren't in any way, "left behind."

The non-Christians are in great tribulation, after they worshipped the beast and his image, and received the mark on their foreheads, on and on their hands.

The non-Christians, or the wicked, are the ones tormented by locusts in Revelation 9. And once the non-Christians, or the wicked, had taken the mark of the beast, and worshipped his image, they break out in a boil, in Revelation 16, and so on.

Revelation 20:3 and cast him into the bottomless pit, and shut him up, and set a seal upon him, that he should deceive the nations no more, till the thousand years should be fulfilled, and after that he must be loosed a little season

Revelation 20:9 And they went up on the breadth of the earth, compassed the camp of the saints, and the beloved city: and fire came down from God out of heaven and devoured them

Revelation 20:10 and the devil that deceived them was cast into the Lake of Fire and brimstone, where the beast and false prophet are, and shall be tormented day and night, forever and ever.

OF NOTE; now we know a little bit about, why the saints were beheaded, and the beast overcomes them and kills them. They were commonly known as deceived.

Deception will bring destruction upon the saints of God. They are deceived and still being deceived, through such false and un-biblical doctrines, such as the so-called rapture. They are also following false prophets.

The Saints of God, will be partially responsible for the antichrist's reign of terror to the whole world, if and when, they bring this beast to power.

Revelation 21:7 He that overcomes shall inherit all things

2 Corinthians 7:4 I am filled with comfort I am exceedingly joyful in all tribulation

2 Peter 2:9 the Lord knows how to deliver the godly out of temptations, and to reserve the unjust unto the day of judgment to be punished

2 Timothy 2:26 And they shall recover themselves out of the snare of the devil, who are taken captive of him at his will

Philippians 1:21 For to me is live in Christ, and to die is gain

Titus 3:3 For we ourselves were sometimes foolish, disobedient, deceived, serving divers lusts, and pleasures, living in malice, and envy, hateful, and hating one another

Daniel 9:5 we have sinned, and committed iniquity, and have done wickedly, and have rebelled, even by departing from the precepts

Matthew 24:5 for many shall come in my name, saying, I am Christ, and shall deceive many

Matthew 24:9 then shall they deliver you up to be afflicted, and then shall kill you: and ye shall be hated of all nations for my name's sake

Revelation 12:7 And there was war in heaven: Michael and his angels fought against the dragon; and the dragon fought and his angels

Chapter Thirteen
Jesus' Second Coming

1 Thessalonians 4:13-17 is about Jesus' second coming, and, the first and second resurrection. Not about any ascension to heaven, and using Jesus Christ as the transporter.

Daniel 7:13 and I saw in the night visions, and behold one like the Son of man came with the clouds of heaven, and come with ancient of days, and brought him near before them

Daniel 7:14 and there was given him dominion, and glory, and a kingdom, that all people nations, and languages, should serve him. His dominion is an everlasting dominion, which shall not pass away, and his kingdom that which shall not be destroyed

Daniel 12:2 And many of them that sleep in the dust of the earth shall awake to everlasting life, some to shame and everlasting contempt

Acts 2:19 And I will show wonders in heaven above and signs in the earth beneath; blood, and fire, and vapor of smoke

Acts 2:20 the sun shall be turned into darkness, and the moon into blood, before that great and notable day of the Lord come

Acts 2:21 And it shall come to pass that whoever call on the name of the Lord shall be saved

Acts 3:20 And he shall send Jesus Christ, which before was preached unto you

Acts 3:21 Whom the heaven must receive until the times of restitution of all things, which God has spoken by the mouth of all his holy prophets since the world began

Acts 1:11 which also said, ye men of Galilee, why stand ye gazing up into heaven?

This same Jesus, which is taken up from you into heaven, so shall come in like manner, as ye have seen him go into heaven

Acts 1:12 Then returned they into Jerusalem from the mount called Olivet, which is from Jerusalem a Sabbath day's journey

Acts 10:42 he commanded us to preach to the people and to testify that is he which was ordained of God to be the judge of the quick and the dead

Acts 24:15 And have hope toward God, which they themselves also allow, there shall be resurrection, both of the just and of the unjust

Zacharias 14:1 Behold, the day of the Lord comes, and thy spoil shall be divided in the midst of thee

Zacharias 14:4 and his feet shall stand on the mount of Olives, which is before Jerusalem on the east; and the mount of Olives shall cleave in the midst thereof toward the east and toward the west, and there shall be a very great valley; and a half mountain shall remove toward the north, and half of it toward the south

A Case In Point: Christ must remain in heaven until all prophesies have been fulfilled

Matthew 16:27 for the Son of man shall come in the glory of his Father with his angels; and he shall reward every man according to his works

Matthew 24:27 for as the lightning comes out of the east and shines even to the west; so shall also the coming of the Son of man

Matthew 24:28 for whosesoever the carcass is, there will the eagles be gathered together

Matthew 24:29 immediately after the tribulation of those days shall the sun be darkened, and the moon shall not give her light, and the stars shall fall from heaven, and the powers of the heaven shall be shaken.

Matthew 24:30 and then shall appear the Son of man is heaven: the Son of man coming in clouds of heaven with power and great glory

Matthew 24:36 But what hour knows no man, no, not the angels of heaven, but my Father only

Matthew 24:50 The lord of that servant shall come in a day when he look not for him, and in an hour he is not aware of

Matthew 24:51 And shall cut him asunder, and

appoint him his portion with the hypocrites: there shall be weeping and gnashing of teeth

Matthew 25:3-5 They that were foolish took their lamps and took no oil with them

Matthew 25:4 But the wise took oil in their vessels with their lamps

Matthew 25:5 while the bridegroom tarried, they all slumbered and slept

Matthew 25:12 but he answered and said, verily I say unto you, I know you not

Matthew 25:13 watch ye therefore, for ye know neither the day nor the hour wherein the Son of man comes

Matthew 25:30 and cast the unprofitable servant into outer darkness: there shall be weeping and gnashing of teeth

Matthew 27:52 And the graves were opened; and many bodies of the saints which slept arose

Mark 14:62 I am and ye shall see the Son of man sitting on the right hand of power….

Mark 16:19 after he had spoken Jesus was received up to heaven

Luke 17:24 for as lighting, that lights out of one part under heaven, shine unto the other part under heaven; so shall also the Son of man be in his day

Luke 17:34 I tell you, in that night there shall be two men in one bed, the one shall be taken, the other left

Luke 12:36 And ye yourselves like unto men that wait for the Lord, when he will return from the wedding; that when he comes and knocks, they may open unto him immediately

Luke 17:35 two women shall be grinding together, the one shall be taken, the other one left

Luke 12:46 the lord of that servant will come in a day when he look not for him, and at an hour when he is not aware, and will cut him in sunder and will appoint him his portion with the unbelievers

Luke 21:25 there shall be signs in the sun, and in the moon, and in the stars; and upon the earth and distress of nations, with perplexity; the sea and the waves roaring

Luke 21:26 Men's hearts failing them for fear, and for looking after those things coming upon the world

Luke 21:27 then shall they see the Son of man coming in a cloud with glory and great power

John 14:3 And if I go and prepare a place for you, I will come again, and receive you unto myself; that where I am, that ye may be also

Romans 9:28 For he will finish the work, and cut it short in righteousness: because a short work will the Lord make upon the earth

A Case In Point: Matthew 25:3-5 the parable of the woman with the lamps, the bridegroom tarried, they all slumbered and slept.

Hebrews 9:28 so Christ was once offered to bear the sins of many; and unto them that look for him shall he appear the second time without sin unto salvation

Hebrews 4:14 Seeing then we have a high priest that is passed into the heavens, Jesus the Son of God, let us hold fast our profession

2 Corinthians 12:4 How that he was caught up into paradise, and heard unspeakable words, which is not lawful for a man to utter

1 Thessalonians 4:15 for if we believe Jesus also died and rose again even so them which are asleep in Jesus will God bring with him

Revelation 19:11 I saw heaven opened, and behold a white horse; and he that sat upon him was called Faithful and True, and in righteousness he does judge and make war

Revelation 19:12 and his eyes were as a flame of fire, and on his head were many crowns; and he had a name written, and that no man knew, but he himself.

Revelation 19:13 And he was clothed in a vesture dipped in blood: and his name is called The Word of God

Revelation 19:14 And the armies which are in heaven followed him upon the white horses, clothed in fine linen, white and clean.

Revelation 19:19 And I saw the beast, and kings

of the earth, and their armies, gathered together to make war against him that sat on the horse, and against his army

Revelation 19:21 And the remnant were slain with the sword of him that sat upon the horse, which sword proceeded out of his mouth: and all the fowls were filled with their flesh

2 Timothy 4:1 I charge you therefore before God and the Lord Jesus Christ who shall judge the quick and the dead at his appearing and his kingdom

1 Thessalonians 4:15 for if we believe Jesus also died and rose again even so then which are asleep in Jesus will God bring with him

2 Thessalonians 2:9 Behold I come quickly my reward is with me

Revelation 22:7 behold I come quickly

Revelation 22:12 and behold I come quickly; and my reward is with me; to give every man according as his work shall be

Revelation 22:20 Surely I come quickly

Hebrews 9:28 so Christ was once offered to bear the sins of many; and unto them that look for him shall he appear the second time without sin unto salvation

Acts 1:11 Which also said, ye men of Galilee, why stand ye gazing into heaven? This same Jesus, taken up from you into heaven, so shall come in like manner as you have seen him go into heaven

Luke 19:37 And when he was come nigh, even at the descent at the mount of Olives, the whole multitude of the disciples began to rejoice and praise God with a loud voice for all the mighty works they had seen

Titus 2:13 Looking for that blessed hope and glorious appearing of the great God and our Savior Jesus Christ

2 Timothy 4:1 I charge you before God, and the Lord Jesus Christ, who shall judge the quick and the dead, at his appearing and his kingdom

1 Corinthians 15:52 in a moment in a twinkling of an eye in the last Trump for them trumpet shall sound and the dead shall be raised incorruptible and we shall all be changed

1 Thessalonians 4:16 For the Lord himself shall descend from heaven with a shout, with the voice of the archangel, and with the trump of God; and the dead in Christ shall rise first

2 Thessalonians 2:9 Behold I come quickly and my reward is with me

Romans 2:16 In the day when God shall judge the secrets of men by Jesus Christ according to my gospel

Ezra 7:10 For Ezra had prepared his heart to seek the law of the Lord, and to do it, and to teach Israel statues and judgment

1 Thessalonians 5:6 But let us not sleep as others

do, but let us watch and be sober

1 Peter 4:7 But the end of all things is at hand: be ye therefore sober, and watch unto prayer

Matthew 24:5 and many shall come in my name, saying, I am Christ and shall deceive many

OF NOTE: Yeshua is a false Christ and messiah, and Yahwe is not the name of God. Genesis 22:14, Matthew 24:24, Psalms 83:18

Chapter Fourteen
All the Prophets Died

John 8:52 then the Jews said into him, now we know that he has a devil, Abraham is dead and the prophets; and thou says, if a man have keep my saying, he shall never see death

John 8:53 Are thou greater than our father Abraham, which is now dead? And the prophets are dead: whom makes thou thyself?

Psalms 89:47 Remember how short my time is: Wherefore has thou made all men in vain?

Psalms 89:48 what man is it that says he shall not see death? Shall he deliver his soul from the hand of the grave?

Psalms 116:15 precious in the sight of the Lord is the death of his saints

John 21:23 which went the saying abroad among the brethren that the disciple should not die, yet Jesus said not unto him, He shall not die; if I will he tarry till I come. What is that to thee?

Luke 2:26 and it was revealed to him by the Holy Ghost, that he should not see death, before he had seen the Lord's Christ

2 Samuel 14:14 for we must needs die, and are as

water spit on the ground, which cannot be gathered up again: neither does God respect any person; yet does he devise means that his banished be not expelled from him

John 6:49 your fathers did eat manna in the wilderness and are dead

Acts 2:29 Men and brethren let me speak freely unto you of the Patriarch David, that he is both dead and buried and his sepulchre is with us unto this day

Acts 2:34 For David is not ascended into heaven: but said of himself, The Lord said unto my Lord, Sit thou on my right hand

Acts 2:35 until I make thy foes thy footstool

Acts 24:15 And we have hope toward God, which they themselves also allow, that there shall be a resurrection of the dead, both of the just and the unjust

Romans 5:12 wherefore, as by one man sin entered into the world, and death by sin; and so death passed upon all men, for that all have sinned

Romans 5:14 nevertheless death reigned from Adam to Moses, even over them that had not sinned after the similitude of Adam's transgression, who is the figure of him that was to come

Romans 6:7 for he that is dead is freed from sin

Romans 6:8 now if we believe we be dead with Christ, we believe we shall also live with him

Romans 6:9 knowing that Christ raised from the dead dies no more; death has no more dominion over him

Romans 6:10 For in that he died, he died unto sin once: but in that he lives, he lives unto God

Romans 6:23 wages of sin is death, but the gift of God is eternal life in Christ Jesus our Lord

Romans 7:9 for I was alive without the law once: but when the commandment came, sin revived, and I died

Romans 7:10 And the commandment, which ordained to life, I found to be unto death

Romans 8:8 So then they that are in the flesh cannot please God

Philippians 1:21 For to me is live in Christ, and to die is gain

1 Corinthians 15:26 the last enemy that shall be destroyed is death

1 Corinthians 15:27 For he has put all things under his feet

1 Corinthians 15:52 I charge you therefore before God and the Lord Jesus Christ who shall judge the quick and the dead at his appearing and his kingdom

1 Corinthians 15:22 for as in Adam all die, even so in Christ shall all be made alive

Hebrews 2:9 Jesus was made a little lower than the angels that he by the grace of God should taste death for every man

Hebrews 2:14 ……that through death he might destroy him that has power of death that is the devil

Hebrews 2:15 and deliver them who through fear of death were all their lifetime subject to bondage

Hebrews 9:27 it is appointed unto man once to die after that the judgment

2 Corinthians 5:10 For we must all appear before the judgment seat of Christ; everyone might receive the things done in his body, according to that he has done, whether it be good or bad

Romans 14:10 but why does thou judge thou brother? Or why does thou set at nought thy brother? But we shall stand before the judgment seat of Christ

Hebrews 9:17 for a testament is of force after men are dead: otherwise it is of no strength at all while the testator lives

Hebrews 11:13 these all died in faith not having received the promise ……..

1 Peter 4:5 where shall give account to him to judge the quick and the dead

Philippians 1:20 according to my expectation and hope, that in nothing I shall be ashamed, that with all boldness, as always, so now also Christ shall be magnified in my body, whether I be by life, or by death

Ecclesiastes 9:5 for the living know that they shall die: but the know not anything, neither have they anymore a reward; for the memory of them is forgotten

Luke 16:19-22 it came to pass that the beggar died, and was carried by the angels into Abraham's bosom: the rich man died also and was buried 16:23 and in hell he lifted up his eyes, being in torments, and sees Abraham afar off, and Lazarus in his bosom

Acts 2:38 then Peter said, Repent ye and be baptized every one of you in the name of Jesus Christ, for the remission of sins and you shall receive the gift of the Holy Ghost

Revelation 2:10 be thou faithful unto death and I will give you the crown of life

Romans 11:3 Lord they have killed thy prophets, and digged down thy altars, and I am left alone, and they seek thy life

1 Thessalonians 2:15 who both killed the Lord Jesus, and their own prophets, and have persecuted us; they please not the Lord, and are contrary to all men

1 kings 18:4 for it was so, when Jezebel cut off the prophets of the Lord, and Obadiah took a hundred prophets and hid them by fifty in a cave, and fed them bread and water

1 Kings 19:1 and Ahab told Jezebel all that Elijah

had done, and withal he had s slain all the prophets with a sword

Matthew 23:37 O Jerusalem, Jerusalem, thou that killed the prophets, and stones them which are sent unto thee, how often would I have gathered thy children together, even as a hen gathers her chickens under her wings and ye would not!

Chapter Fifteen
John 17:15

John 17:4 I have glorified thee on earth: I have finished the work, thou gave me to do

John 17:10 All mine are thine, and thine are mine; and I am glorified in them

Psalms 37:28 for the Lord loves judgment and forsakes not his saints; for they are preserved forever

Acts 2:27 because thou will not leave my soul in hell, nor will thou suffer thine Holy One to see corruption

A Case In Point: Do not take them before the work is done, is what John is saying in this verse to the Father

John 17:15 I pray not that thou should take them out of the world, but that thou should keep them from evil

John 17:16 they are not of the world, even as I am not of the world;

John 17:17 sanctify them through thy truth: thy word is truth

John 17:18 As thou has sent me into the world, even so have I also sent them into the world

John 17:19 And for their sakes I sanctify myself, that they also may be sanctified through the truth

John 17:20 Neither I pray for these alone, but for them also which shall believe on me through their word

John 17:21 that they all may be one; as thou Father, are in me, and I in thee, that they also may be one in us; that the world may believe that thou has sent me

John 17:22 and the glory which thou gave me I have given them; that they may be one, even as we are one

John 17:23 I in them, and thou in me, that they may be made perfect in one; and that the world may know that thou has sent me, and thou has loved them, as thou has loved me

Philippians 1:29 for unto you it is given in behalf of Christ, not only to believe on him, but to suffer for his sake

1 Chronicles 4:10 And Jabez called on the God of Israel, saying, Oh that thou would bless me indeed, and enlarge my coast, and that thine hand may be with me, and that thou would keep me from evil, that it may not grieve me! And God granted him that which was he requested

Genesis 48:16 and the angel redeemed me from all evil, bless the lads……..

Psalms 121:3 He will not suffer thy foot to be

moved: he that keep thee will not slumber

Psalms 121:4 Behold, he that keeps Israel shall not slumber nor sleep

Psalms 121:5 The Lord is my keeper: The Lord is thy shade upon thy right hand

Psalms 121:6 the sun shall not smite thee by day, nor the moon by day.

A Case In Point: Revelation 16:8 and the fourth angel poured out his vial upon the sun; and power was given him to scorch men with fire

Revelation 16:9 And men were scorched with great heat, and blasphemed the name of God, which had power over all these plagues: and they repented not to give him glory

Psalms 121:7 the Lord shall preserve thee from all evil: he shall preserve thy soul

Psalms 121:8 the Lord shall preserve thy going out and thy coming in from this time forth, and even for evermore

Matthew 6:13 And lead us not into temptation but deliver us from evil…..

Galatians 1:4 who gave himself for our sins, that he might deliver us from the present evil world, according to the will of God and our Father

2 Thessalonians 3:3 But the Lord is faithful, who will stablish you and keep you from evil

1 John 2:13 I write unto you. Fathers, because ye have known him that is from the beginning. I write

unto you, young men, because you have overcome the wicked one, I write unto you, little children, because you have known the Father

1 John 5:18 we know whosoever is born of God sins not; but he that is begotten of God keeps himself, and that wicked one touches him not

1 John 5:19 And we know that we are of God, and the whole world lies in wickedness

Revelation 3:10 Because thou has kept the word of my patience, I also will keep thee from the hour of temptation, which shall come upon all the world, to try them that dwell upon the earth

Luke 24:38 why are ye troubled? and why do thoughts arise in your hearts?

Luke 10:19 I give you power to tread on serpents and scorpions, and over all the power of the enemy, and nothing by any means hurt you

A Case In Point: Revelation 9:3 there came out of the smoke locusts upon the earth: and unto them was given power, as the scorpions of the earth have power. 9:5 …and their torment was as the torment of a scorpion, when he strikes a man

1 Peter 3:13 and who is he that will harm you, if ye be followers of that which is good

2 Peter 2:9 the Lord knows how to deliver the godly out of temptations, and reserve the unjust unto the day of judgment to be punished

Mark 13:13 and ye shall be hated of all men for

my name's sake, and he that shall endure unto the end, the same shall be saved

1 Corinthians 10:13 there is no temptation out of such as it is common to man, but God is faithful who will not suffer you to be tempted above that you are able; but will with the temptation also make a way to escape, that ye may be able to bear it

2 Timothy 4:8 henceforth there is laid up for me a crown of righteousness, which the Lord, the righteous judge, shall give me at that day: and not to me only, but unto them that also love his appearance

2 Timothy 2:26 they shall recover themselves out of the snare of the devil, who are taken captive by him at his will

Isaiah 57:1 the righteous perish and no man lays it to heart; and merciful men are taken away, none considers that the righteous is taken away from the evil to come

2 Kings 22:20 behold therefore, I will gather thee unto thy fathers, and thou shall be gathered unto thy grave in peace; and thine eyes shall not see all the evil which I will bring upon this place. And they brought the king word again

Revelation 2:25 But that which ye have already, hold fast till I come

Revelation 2:26 and he that overcomes and keep my works unto the end, to him will I give power over all the nations

Revelation 3:11 Behold I come quickly: hold that fast which thou has, that no man take thy crown

Revelation 7:3 Saying, Hurt not the earth, neither the sea, nor the trees, till we have sealed the servants of God in our foreheads

Revelation 13:6 and he opened his mouth in blasphemy against God, blaspheme his name, and his tabernacle, and them that dwell in heaven

Revelation 13:7 And it was given unto him to make war with the saints, and to overcome them: and power was given him over all kindred, and tongues and nations

Revelation 13:8 And all that dwell upon the earth shall worship him, whose names are not written in the book of Life of the Lamb slain from the foundation of the world

Chapter Sixteen
No One Has Seen God And Lived

Exodus 3:2 and the angel of the Lord appeared unto him in a flame of fire out of the midst of a bush: and he looked, and, behold, the bush burned with fire, and the bush was not consumed

Exodus 3:3 And Moses said, I will now turn aside, and see this great sight, why the bush is not burnt

Exodus 3:4 And when the Lord saw he turned aside to see, God called him out of the midst of the bush, and said, Moses, Moses. And he said, Here am I.

Exodus 3:5 And he said, Draw not nigh hither: Put off thy shoes from off thy feet, for the place whereon thou stand is holy ground

Exodus 3:6 Moreover he said, I am the God of thy father, the God of Abraham, the God of Isaac, and the God of Jacob. And Moses hid his face; for he was afraid to look on

If Moses had 'looked on,' he would have died right on the spot!

Deuteronomy 4:12 And the Lord spoke unto you out of the midst of the fire: ye heard the voice of the words, but saw no similitude; only ye heard a voice

Exodus 33:20 And he said, Thou cannot see my face: for there can no man see me and live

Colossians 1:15 Who is the image of the invisible God, the firstborn of every creature?

Hebrews 12:14 follow peace with all men, and holiness without which no man shall see the Lord

Job 19:26 And though after my skin worms destroy this body, yet in my flesh shall I see God

Job 19:27 Whom I shall see for myself, and mine eyes shall behold, and not another; though my reins be consumed within me

John 1:18 No man has seen God at any time, the only begotten son, which is in the bosom, of the Father, he has declared him

John 6:46 not that any man has seen the Father, save which he is of God, he has seen the Father

1 John 4:12 no man has seen God at any time......

John 5:37 And he Father himself which sent me, has borne witness of me. Ye have neither heard his voice, any time, nor seen his shape.

Chapter Seventeen
People are in Heaven

Psalms 89:6 who in heaven can be compared to the Lord?

Nehemiah 2:4 then the king said to me, For what does thou make request? So, I prayed to the God of heaven

Ezra 7:21 …..the scribe of the law of the God of heaven

Daniel 2:37 thou O king, are a king of kings; For the God of heaven has given thee a kingdom, power, strength, and glory

Matthew 6:9 Our Father which are in heaven, Hallowed by thy name

Matthew 8:11 I say, unto you, that many shall come from the east, and west, and shall sit down with Abraham, Isaac, and Jacob, in the kingdom of heaven

Matthew 8:12 but the children of the kingdom shall be cast into outer darkness: there shall be weeping and gnashing of teeth

Luke 10:20 notwithstanding in this rejoice not that the spirits are subject unto you; but rather rejoice, because your names are written in heaven

Luke 16:23 And in hell, he lifted up his eyes, being in torments, and sees Abraham afar off, and Lazarus in his bosom

Luke 16:22 it came to pass the beggar died and carried by the angels into Abraham's bosom. The rich man died also and was buried

Matthew 7:38 the two thieves crucified with him, one on the right, the other on the left

Luke 23:43 verily, I say unto thee, Today thou shall be with me in paradise

John 14:2 in my Father's house are many mansions: if it were not so, I would have told you. I go prepare a place for you

John 14:3 and if I go and prepare a place for you, I will come again and receive you unto myself; that where I am, there ye may be also

Hebrews 12:23 to the general assembly and church of the first born who were entered into heaven, and God the judge, and to the spirits of just men made perfect

2 Corinthians 5:8 we are confident I say, and willing rather to be absent from the body, and to be present with the Lord

Revelation 5:3 no man in heaven was able to open the book, nor in earth, neither under the earth, was able to open the book, or to look thereon

Revelation 3:12 he that overcomes will I make a pillar in the temple of my God, and he shall go no more out: and I will write upon him the name of my God, and the name of the city of my God, which is new Jerusalem, which come down out of heaven from my God: and I will write him my new name

Revelation 8:3 another angel came and stood at the altar, having a golden censer; and there was given unto him much incense, that he should offer it with prayers of all saints upon the golden altar which was before the throne

Revelation 14:6 I saw another angel fly in the midst of heaven …..

Revelation 18:1 I saw another angel come down from heaven…...

Revelation 19:1 I heard a great voice of much people in heaven.....

1 Thessalonians 4:13 I would not have you ignorant brethren, concerning them which are asleep in Jesus will God bring with him

OF NOTE; God will bring back, the saints which died in Christ, and are already in heaven, and were raised up in the first resurrection.

Revelation 19:17 I saw an angel standing in the sun; and he cried with a loud voice, saying to all the fowls that fly around in the midst of heaven

Revelation 5:13 and every creature which is in heaven and on the earth, and under the earth, as such as are in the sea…….

Revelation 13:7 And it was given him to make

war with the saints, and overcome them, and power was given over all kindreds, and tongues and nations

Chapter Eighteen
Lazarus, Paul, and John the Baptist

OF NOTE: The soul does not die, or perish, when in death. The Souls of the first, resurrected-dead Christian, goes up to God's kingdom, the heaven of heavens, when they see death.

When Christ returns in 1 Thessalonians 4:13-17, the souls of the first, resurrected-dead saints, will be reunited with their earthly flesh. This is how you answer: if the dead are already in heaven, how is it, they reunite with their earthly flesh, or their former bodies?

In other words, how do they rise from the dead?

2 Corinthians 5:8 we are confident I say, willing to be absent from the body, and to be present with the Lord

Luke 23:43 verily, I say unto thee, Today shall thou be with me in paradise

1 Corinthians 15:51 Behold, I show you a mystery, we shall not all die, but we shall all be changed

1 Corinthians 15:52 in the moment, in the twinkling of an eye, at the last trump; for the trumpet shall sound, and the dead shall be raised

incorruptible, and we shall be changed

OF NOTE: The last trump doesn't sound until Revelation 10:7

Revelation 8:2 and I saw the seven angels which stood before God; and to them were given seven trumpets

OF NOTE: you will be dead in Christ, to be changed.

Exodus 33:20 no man can see God and live

2 Timothy 4:1 I charge thee therefore before God to judge the quick and the dead, at his appearing and his kingdom

1 Peter 4:5 who shall give account to judge the quick and the dead

Revelation 3:2 be watchful and strengthen the things which remain, that are ready to die: for I have not found thy works perfect before God

OF NOTE: 'remain,' can also be found in 1 Thessalonians 4:13-17

Ezra 7:10 For Ezra had prepared his heart to seek the law of the Lord, and to do it, and to teach in Israel statues and judgments

OF NOTE; before Christ's second coming, you must be ready to meet God, by preparing your heart, and before the first resurrection of the dead

1 Corinthians 15:22 For as in a day all men died, even so in Christ shall all men live

2 Corinthians 5:10 For we must all appear before

the judgment seat of Christ; that everyone may receive the things done in his body, according to that he has done, whether it be good or bad

Philippians 1:23 For I am in a strait betwixt two, having a desire to depart, to be with Christ; which is far better

John 11:23 Jesus said to her, thou brother shall rise again

John 11:24 Martha said unto him, I know that he shall rise again in the resurrection at the last day

John 11:25 Jesus said unto her, I am the resurrection, and the life; he that believes in me, though he were dead, yet shall he live

John 11:26 and whosoever lives shall never die, and believes in me. Believe thou this?

John 11:43 when he had thus spoken, he cried with a loud voice, Lazarus come forth

John 11:44 he that was dead came forth bound hand and foot with grave clothes Loose him and let him go

Job 6:63 it is the spirit that quickens the flesh, the flesh profits nothing

OF NOTE: It was necessary for Lazarus to be raised again, because he died in sin, his earthly flesh. Lazarus had to repeat the death process, so that he could be raised incorruptible, in order for him to receive a new body, free of abnormalities or defects.

Romans 6:6 knowing this that our old man is crucified that the body of sin is destroyed, that henceforth we should not serve sin

Romans 8:8 so then they that are in the flesh cannot please God

Romans 8:13 For if ye live after the flesh, ye shall die: but if ye through the Spirit do mortify the deeds of the body, ye shall live

Romans 7:5 For when we were in the flesh, the motions of sins, which were by the law, did work in our members to bring forth fruit unto life

Romans 6:23 For the wages of sin is death, but the gift of God is eternal life in Christ Jesus our Lord

Galatians 6:8 for he that sows to his flesh, shall of the flesh reap corruption; but he that sows in the Spirit shall of the Spirit reap everlasting

Philippians 1:22 But if I live in the flesh, this is the fruit of my labour; yet what I shall choose I wot not

Acts 2:29 men and brethren, let me freely speak to you of the patriarch David, that he is both dead and buried, and his sepulchre is with us unto this day

Acts 2:34 For David is not ascended into the heavens……

Matthew 14:2 at that time Herod the tetrarch heard the fame of Jesus

Matthew 14:3 For Herod laid hold on John and

bound him, and put him in a prison for Herodias' sake, his brother Philip's wife

Matthew 14:4 For John said unto him, it is not lawful for him to have her

Matthew 14:8 And she being instructed of her mother, said, Give me here John the Baptist's head in a charger

Luke 9:7 now Herod the tetrarch heard all that was done by him: and he was perplexed, because that it was said of some, that John was risen from the dead

Luke 9:8 And of some, that Elias had appeared, and of others, that one of the old prophets was risen again

Luke 9:9 And Herod said, John, have I beheaded: but who is this, of whom I hear such things? And he desired to see him

Luke 9:19 They answering said, John the Baptist, but some say, Elias; and others say, that one of the old prophets is risen again

OF NOTE: Lazarus, Paul, and John The Baptist, were not 'received,' into heaven, as was Jesus' ascension into God's kingdom. Philip and the two witnesses of Revelation, were not 'received,' into heaven, and neither, were carried away by angels.

Chapter Nineteen
Revelation 3:2

Ezra 7:10 For Ezra had prepared his heart to seek the law of the Lord, and to do it, and to teach Israel statues and judgment

Daniel 12:2 And many of them that sleep in the dust of the earth shall awake, some to everlasting life, some to shame and everlasting contempt

2 Timothy 4:1 I charge you therefore before God and the Lord Jesus Christ who shall judge the quick and the dead at his appearing and his kingdom

1 Peter 4:5 Who shall give account to him to judge the quick and the dead

1 Thessalonians 4:13 but I would not have you ignorant brethren concerning them which are asleep, that ye sorrow not, even as others which have no hope

1 Thessalonians 4:14 For if we believe that Jesus died and rose again even also them also which sleep in Jesus will God bring with him

1 Thessalonians 4:15 For this I say unto you by the word of the Lord that we which are alive and remain shall unto the coming of the Lord shall not prevent them which are asleep

1 Thessalonians 4:16 For the Lord himself shall descend from heaven with a shout, with the voice of the archangel, and with the trump of God: and the dead in Christ shall rise first

1 Thessalonians 4:17 Then we which are alive and remain shall be caught up together with them in the clouds to meet the Lord in the air, so shall we ever be with the Lord

1 Peter 4:5 who shall give account to him that is ready to judge the quick and the dead

1 Peter 4:7 but the end of all things is at hand: be ye therefore sober, and watch unto prayer

1 Thessalonians 5:6 But let us not sleep, as others do, but let us watch and be sober

1 Corinthians 15:52 In a moment, in a twinkling of an eye, in the last trump, for the trump shall sound, and the dead shall be raised incorruptible, and we shall all be changed

Revelation 2:4 nevertheless I have somewhat against thee, because thou has left thy first love

Revelation 3:1 and to the angels of the church in Sardis write …. I know thy works and thou are dead

Chapter Twenty
The Rapture and Left Behind Lies

The word origins for rapture are "snatched," "seized," "taken away," gasp! "raped." Yes, the term, "rapture," is an ancient African term for rape. This dates back to the 1600's.

If you, or someone else, were victimized by one of these terms, you wouldn't call it "raptured,"

No one in the biblical sense was victimized by being "snatched," "seized," "raped," or forcibly "taken away," from the earth to heaven.

"Taken away," is not the same as "taken up,"

"Catching away," is not the same as "caught up."

"Caught up," is not a word origin for "rapture." "Catching away," is not a logical word origin for forcing one to do anything. One definition for "rapture," is taken someone, or object, by force.

If you were duped by the work of fiction, titled, 'Left Behind,' written by Tim Lahaye, you are not alone.

The term rapture dates back to the year 1832, when an ailing woman, by the name of Margaret McDonald, on her dying bed, claimed to have "raptured -up." So, we know, that the practice isn't biblical.

Romans 16:17 now I beseech you, brethren, mark them which cause divisions and offences contrary to the doctrine which ye have learned: and avoid them

1 Timothy 4:2 speaking lies in hypocrisy, having their conscience seared with a hot iron

2 Timothy 4:2 Preach the word; be instant in season, out of season; reprove, rebuke, exhort with all longsuffering and doctrine

2 Timothy 4:3 For the time will come, when they will not endure sound doctrine; but after their own lusts shall heap to themselves teachers, having itching ears

1 Corinthians 14:33 For God is not the author of confusion, but of peace, but in all churches of the saints

Deuteronomy 29:29 the secrets things belong unto the Lord our Lord, but those things which are revealed belong to us and to our children forever, that we may all do the words of the law

2 Timothy 3:13 but evil men shall wax worse and worse, deceived and being deceived

Titus 3:3 we ourselves were sometimes foolish, disobedient, deceived, serving divers lusts and pleasures, living in malice and envy, hateful, and hating one another

Ezekiel 14:9 and the prophet he deceived when

he had spoken a thing, I the Lord have deceived the prophet, and I will stretch out my hand upon him, and will destroy him from the midst of my people Israel

Revelation 11:3 I will give power unto my two witnesses, they shall prophesy a thousand and two hundred and threescore days, clothed in sackcloth

Revelation 17:8 I saw the woman drunken with blood of the saints, an with the blood of the martyrs of Jesus

Revelation 18:24 and in her was found the blood of the prophets, an of saints and all that was slain upon the earth

Revelation 20:4 ….and I saw the souls of them that were beheaded for the witness of Jesus, and for the word of God, which had not worshipped the beast, neither his image, nor had received his mark upon their foreheads, or in their hands; and they lived and reigned with Christ a thousand years

Revelation 22:15 For without are dogs, and sorcerers, and whoremongers, and murderers, and idolaters, and whosoever loves and makes a lie.

Revelation 14:1 And I looked and lo a Lamb stood on the mount Sion, and with him a hundred and forty and four thousand, having his Father's name written in their foreheads

Revelation 14:4 these are they which are not defiled with women; for they are virgins. These are they which follow the Lamb withers ever he goes. These were redeemed from among men, being the first fruits unto God and to the Lamb

Revelation 14:5 and in their mouth was found no guile: for they are without fault before the throne of God

Mark 14:62 And Jesus said, I am: and ye shall see Son of man sitting on the right hand of power coming in clouds of heaven

OF NOTE; You will see Christ coming with your own eyes.

Revelation 18:24 And in her was found the blood of the prophets, and of saints, and all that was slain upon the earth

OF NOTE: These saints were not "Left Behind."

Genesis 6:8 Found grace in the eyes of the Lord.

Genesis 6:9 Noah was a just man, perfect in his generation, and Noah walked with God

OF NOTE: The same as Enoch, Noah walked with God, but yet, Noah remained upon the earth, while, Enoch was translated.

Genesis 6:12 God looked upon the earth and behold it was corrupt; For all flesh had corrupted his way upon the earth

Genesis 6:13 the end of all flesh is come before me……..

Genesis 6:14 make thee an ark of gopher wood....

Genesis 6:17 and, behold, I even I, do bring a flood of waters, to destroy all flesh, wherein is the breath of life, from under heaven, and everything that is in the earth shall die.

Genesis 7:21 and all the flesh died that moved upon the earth, both of food and of cattle, and of beast, and of every creeping thing, that creeps upon the earth, and every man died

Genesis 7:22 and in whose nostrils was breath of life, of all that was in the land, died

2 Peter 2:5 And spared not the old world, but saved Noah, he eighth person, a preacher of righteousness, bringing in the flood upon the world of the ungodly

OF NOTE: Noah wasn't translated, or ascended into the heavens, instead, Noah and his family were left to repopulate the earth again. And because, Noah was not lifted up anywhere, he also saved the animals that existed, and brought them back to existence. Had they been taken off the earth, and not 'left behind," there would have been no population on earth, or any animals in existence.

Noah did not perish in the flood waters, and God provided a way for Noah and family to escape, without leaving the earth. The ones lost, were the individuals, which drowned in the flood waters. The ones, "left behind, "Noah, and family, were not of the "unsaved," or 'non-Christians."

Genesis 18:20 and the Lord said, Because the cry of Sodom and Gomorrah is very great, and because their sins is very grievous

Genesis 18:23 will thou destroy the righteous with the wicked?

Genesis 18:33 and the Lord went his way, as soon as he left commuting with Abraham, and Abraham returned to his place

Genesis 19:1 there came two angels at Sodom at even; and Lot sat in the gate at Sodom: and Lot seeing them rose up to meet them, he bowed his face toward the ground

Genesis 19:13 But we will destroy this place, Because the cry of them is waxen great before the face of the Lord; and the Lord sent us to destroy it

Genesis 19:17 …..escape for thy life, look not behind thee, neither stay thee in all the plains; escape to all the mountain, lest thou be consumed

Genesis 17:19 and I cannot escape to the mountain, and some evil take me, and I die

Genesis 17:34 …..and go thou in and lie with him to preserve seed of my father

2 Peter 2:6 turning the cities of Sodom and Gomorrah into ashes condemned them with an overthrow, making them an ensample unto those that should live ungodly

2 Peter 2:7 and delivered just Lot, vexed with the filthy conversation of the wicked

OF NOTE: Lot was left behind, but not ascended up into the heavens, instead, he was left on earth to preserve life. Also, the ones taken, were the "unsaved," cities of Sodom and Gomorrah

Genesis 50:20 But as for you, you thought evil against me; but God meant it unto good, to bring it to pass, as it is this day, to bring much people alive

OF NOTE; Joseph was left behind, when he was stowed away from Egypt, Joseph was not a non-Christian, or 'unsaved." By not ascending into the heavens, Joseph preserved life, while not exiting the earth.

Job 1:1 There was a man in the land of Uz, whose name was Job; and that man was perfect and upright, one that feared God, and eschewed evil

Job 1:12 And the Lord said unto Satan, Behold, all that he has is in thy power; only upon himself, put not forth thine hand. So Satan went forth from the presence of the Lord

OF NOTE: Job suffered pain and suffering, after he was handed over to the devil Job 16:11

OF NOTE; Job's former family were all taken, Job was 'left behind," Job was not, non-Christian, and yet, he endured pain, suffering and tribulation.

2 Corinthians 12:1 It is not expedient for me doubtless to glory, I will come to visions and revelations of the Lord

2 Corinthians 12:2 I knew a man in Christ above

fourteen years ago (whether in the body, I cannot tell; or whether out of the body, I cannot tell: God knows, such an one caught up to the third heaven

2 Corinthians 12:3 and I knew such a man (whether in the body (whether in the body, or out of the body, I cannot tell: God knows)

2 Corinthians 12:4 How that he was caught up into paradise, and heard unspeakable words, which is not lawful for a man to utter

2 Corinthians 12:5 such an one I will not glory: yet of myself, I will not glory, but in mine infirmities

2 Corinthians 12:7 lest I should be exalted above measure through the abundance of all revelations, there was given to me a thorn in the flesh, the messenger of Satan to buffet me, lest I should be exalted above measure

2 Corinthians 12:8 For this thing I besought the Lord thrice, that it might depart from me

Revelation 14:1 And I looked, and lo, a Lamb stood on the mount Sion, and with him a hundred and forty four thousand, having his Father's name written in their foreheads

Revelation 14:4 and they were not defiled with women; for they are virgins. These are they which follow the Lamb withers ever he goes. These were redeemed from among men, being the first fruits unto God and to the Lamb

Revelation 14:5 and in their mouth was found

no guile: for they are without fault before the throne of God

OF NOTE; the one hundred and forty four thousand, are not among the non-Christians, that are "Left Behind." The one hundred and forty four thousand, are also in the midst of the great tribulation. They have not left the earth in a "rapture," or ascended anywhere.

The one hundred and forty four thousand, are without any faults. So, they are not the "unsaved," that have yet to accept Christ. They had always accepted God.

Revelation 19:21 and the remnant were slain with the sword of him that sat upon the horse

Revelations 20:4 I saw the souls of them beheaded for the witness of Jesus, and for the word of God, and which had not worshipped the beast, neither his image, neither had received his mark upon their foreheads, or in their hands; and they lived and reigned with Christ a thousand years.

OF NOTE; Revelation 20:4 is not talking about the "new Christians," of whom, were "unsaved," and had not come to accept Christ. These are the saints of God, who didn't violate the laws of God. In other words, these are not the "unsaved," classified, as the "Left Behind," of whom, never accepted Jesus Christ as their Lord and Savior.

Nevertheless these saints, are in the latter, great

tribulation, are killed, or beheaded, the same as anyone else. They are treated no differently, than the "unsaved," or non-Christians, and the wicked, by the antichrist. And besides, the antichrist makes war with the saints to overcome them. He doesn't make war with anyone else.

Even after he comes into power, through their support, he will turn against them.

Revelation 18:24 And in her was found the blood of the prophets, and of saints, and all that was slain upon the earth

Numbers 16:6 take ye censers, Korah, and all his company

Numbers 16:7 And put fire therein, and put incense in them before the Lord tomorrow; and it shall be that the man whom the Lord does choose, he shall be holy: ye take too much upon you ye sons of Levi

Numbers 16:8 Moses said to Korah, Hear I pray you, ye sons of Levi

Numbers 16:11 for which cause both thou and all thy company are gathered together against the Lord: And what is Aaron that ye murmur against him?

Numbers 16:18 they took every man his censer, and put fire in them, and laid incense thereon, and stood in the door of the tabernacle of the congregation with Moses and Aaron

Numbers 16:20 the Lord spoke to Moses and unto Aaron

Numbers 16:21 Separate yourselves from among this congregation

Numbers 16:26 Depart from the tents of these wicked men, and touch nothing of theirs lest ye be consumed in all their sins

Numbers 16:27 ……Abiram and Dathan came out, and stood in the door of their tents and their wives, and their sons, and their little children

Numbers 16:30 if the Lord make a new thing, and the earth open her mouth, and swallow them up, with all that appertain to them, and they go down quick into the pit: then ye shall understand these men provoke the Lord

Numbers 16:31 it came to pass, as he had made an end of speaking all these words, that the ground clave asunder that was under them

Numbers 16:32 and the earth opened her mouth and swallowed them up, and their houses, and all the men that appertained unto Korah, and all their goods

Numbers 16:33 They, and all that appertained unto them, went down alive into the pit, and the earth closed upon them: and they perished from among the congregation

Numbers 16:34 and all Israel that were round about them fled at the cry of them: for they said,

Lest the earth swallow us up also

Numbers 16:35 And there came out a fire from the Lord, and consumed the two hundred and fifty men that offered incense

OF NOTE; Do not offer strange sacrifices, beliefs, teachings, sermons, doctrines, mysticism, ecstasy, heresy, and other unlawful, practices to the Lord

Proponents of a "rapture," are the, "rapture nuts are hard to crack." Usually, they are of the heathens, infidel, the unholy, unsaved, sects, polygamists, mystics, and far east religious practices, 2 Corinthians 6:15 and what concord has Christ with Belial? Or what part has he with an infidel?

The whole concept of a "rapture," is inconsistent with Holy Bible scriptures, and prophesy, in either the Old and New Testament, of the Holy Bible.

Matthew 7:15 Beware of false prophets, which come to you in sheep clothing, outwardly, they are ravening wolves

Matthew 24:24 For false messiahs and false prophets will appear and perform great signs and wonders to deceive, if possible the very elect

Matthew 24:11 and many false prophets shall rise, and shall deceive many

2 Peter 2:1 But there were false prophets also among the people, even as there shall be false teachers among you, who privily shall bring in

damnable heresies, even denying the Lord that bought them, and bring among themselves swift destruction

2 Peter 2:2 and many shall follow their pernicious ways; by reason of whom the way of truth shall be evil spoken of

2 Peter 2:3 and through covetousness make merchandise of you: whose judgment now of a long time lingers not and their damnation slumbers not

OF NOTE: there were many duped into purchasing and reading articles, by Tim LaHaye

False prophets, that come to preach "rapture," are "full of signs, and lying wonders, "2 Thessalonians 2:9

False prophets therefore preaches a "rapture," to their congregations, and audiences, are into self-indulgences, fame and fortune, popularity, most of all they are pulling a scam to collect funds for their own benefit, and or, their organizations. While they see it for a good cause, and to deceive the Christians, so they feel completely exonerated, and justified in the behavior.

The congregations of these false prophets, leave with the satisfaction, that their fantasy, delusions, can come true, and they won't have to fear, and suffer through the great tribulation. A "rapture," doctrine is peace and security for them.

Amos 5:19 As a man did flee from the lion, and a

bear met him, or went into the house, and leaned his hand on the wall and a serpent bite him

Jeremiah 48:44 He that flees from the fear shall fall into the pit; and he that gets up out of the pit shall be taken in a snare….

Isaiah 24:18 and it shall come to pass, that he who flees from the noise of the fear shall fall into the pit; and he that comes up out of the midst of the pit shall be taken in a snare: for the windows from on high are open and the earth do shake

Lamentations 3:47 Fear and a snare is come upon us, desolation and destruction

Revelation 2:2 I know thy works and thy labor, and thy patience, and how thou cannot bear them which are evil: and thou has tried them which say they are apostles, and are not, and found them liars

Revelation 21:8 but the fearful, and unbelieving, and all the abominable, and murders, and whoremongers, and sorcerers, and idolaters, and al liars, shall have their part in the lake which burn fire and brimstone, which is the second death

Some of these false prophets, have abased and exalted themselves, into thinking, they can do no wrong.

Luke 6:26 Woe unto you, when men shall speak well of you! For so did their fathers to the false prophets

1 John 4:1 Dear friends do not believe every

spirit but test the spirits to see whether they are from God, because many false prophets are gone out into the world

John 17:15 I pray not that thou take them out of the world, but that thou keep them from evil

Jeremiah 23:16 thus said the Lord of hosts

Hearken not unto the words of the prophets that prophesy unto you: they make you vain: they speak a vision of their own heart, and not out of the mouth of the Lord

OF NOTE: The "rapture," is false hope

Ephesians 5:8 you were sometimes in darkness, but now are you a light in the Lord

2 Corinthians 6:15 do not be unequally bound with unbelievers, or how can light have fellowship with darkness

Ephesians 5:6 Let no man deceive you with vain words: for because of these things comes the wrath of God upon the children of disobedience

Ephesians 5:11 and have no fellowship with unfruitful works of darkness

Psalms 106:35 but were mingled among the heathen and learned their works

Isaiah 57:1 the righteous perish and no man lays it to heart: and merciful men are taken away, none considering that the righteous is taken away from the evil to come

OF NOTE: the righteous doesn't perish forever,

if he has righteousness in Christ. Jesus Christ will give him peace, rest, and security. The righteous will be delivered from all troubles. 1 Corinthians 15:55 O death, where is thy sting? O death, where is thy victory?

1 Corinthians 15:57 but thanks be to God which gives us victory through our Lord Jesus Christ

OF NOTE: the righteous is delivered from the sting of death, and not the stroke of death. He perishes as the outward man, and never in Jesus Christ

Ecclesiastes 7:15 all things have I seen in the days of my vanity: there is a just man that perishes in his righteousness, and there is a wicked man who prolongs his life, in his wickedness

Ecclesiastes 8:14 There is vanity which is done upon the earth; that be just men, unto whom it happen according to the work of the wicked; again, there be wicked men, to whom it happens according to the work of the righteous: I said that this is also vanity

2 Kings 22:20 behold therefore, I will gather thee to thy fathers, and thou shall be gathered to the grave in peace, and thou shall not see all the evil which I will bring upon this place. And they brought the king word again

OF NOTE: Josiah died a premature death, by not growing old

1 Corinthians 10:13 there has no temptations taken you but such as is common to man: but God is faithful, who will not suffer you to be tempted above all that which ye are able; but will also with the temptation make a way to escape, that ye may be able to bear it

Matthew 24:5 For many shall come in my name, saying, I am Christ to deceive many

Chapter Twenty-One
The Rapture a is Moot Point

The dead will not meet God in the air. The resurrected-raised -dead are already in heaven, when Christ returns,

A rapture isn't spiritual, biblical, or physically possible. "You can't get there from here," as the saying goes.

The Second resurrected dead, are separated from God, eternally. So, they won't meet Christ at his second coming.

Only those in the first resurrection, will Christ bring with him, not meeting him.

And after you met him, you won't be returning with him alive, or dead, either.

No one ever ascended into heaven with Jesus Christ.

John 3:13 and no man as ascended up to heaven, but he that came down from heaven, even the Son of man which is in heaven

Since Jesus Christ isn't scheduled to return until, immediately after the great tribulation, so what is the point?

Since, no one can see God and live, you won't be

meeting him face -to- face, either.

It's impossible to meet God in the air, while still living and breathing, in the flesh.

Exodus 33:20 Thou cannot see my face, for there can no man see me and live

John 1:18 no man has seen God at any time….

"No man,' as in, Enoch, Elijah, et al.,

John 3:13 no man has ascended up to heaven, but he that came down from heaven, even the Son of man which is in heaven

John 17:15 I pray not that thou should take them out of the world, but that thou should keep them from evil

1 Thessalonians 4:13-17 and 1 Corinthians 15:51, and 1 Corinthians 15:52 cannot be taken face value

You are highly unlikely to meet God, in the air, in the flesh Romans 8:8 so then they that are in the flesh cannot please God

Neither of the popular scriptures for the "rapture," says that, anyone can ascend into heaven, alive or dead.

Paul had a vision, that he was caught up to the third heaven into paradise. Paul did not ascend into heaven alive, or in the flesh.

In fact, Paul admonished himself in 2 Corinthians 2:7 for thinking that way.

Revelation 3:2 scriptures like this one makes the "rapture," heresy, null and void

Elijah and Enoch, were either translated, or went up to the heavens, 'alive.'

We know at least, that neither, Enoch nor Elijah, made it into heaven, when they were translated, or went up.

And because of that, they were alive, John 1:8 says, they didn't see God, so, it's moot point.

John The Baptist was confused with Jesus Christ, by king Herod, and others.

OF NOTE: There shall be no reversal for the rapture doctrine. God will not take back his word. Revelation 22:18-19 Isaiah 55:10 For as the rain comes down, and the snow from heaven, returns not hither, but waters the earth, and make it bring forth and bud, that it may give seed to the sower, and bread to the eater

Isaiah 40:8 the grass withers, the flower fades: but the word of our God shall stand forever

Isaiah 45:23 I have sworn by myself, the words have gone out of my mouth in righteousness, and it shall not return, that unto me, every knee shall bow, every tongue swear

Isaiah 55:11 So shall my word be that goes forth out of my mouth: it shall not return unto me void, but it shall accomplish that which I please, and it shall prosper in the thing whereto I sent it

Jeremiah 23:20 The anger of the Lord shall not return, until he have executed. And till he have performed, the thoughts of his heart: in the latter days ye shall consider it perfectly

Matthew 24:35 Heaven and earth shall pass away, but my words shall not pass away

Numbers 23:19 God is not a man, that he should lie; neither the Son of man that he should repent

Chapter Twenty-Two
Surviving the Great Tribulation

Revelation 7:3 Saying, Hurt not the earth,
 neither the sea, nor the trees, till we have sealed the servants of our God in their foreheads

Revelation 9:4 ..have the seal of God I their foreheads

Revelation 2:10 ....be thou faithful unto death and I will give you the crown of life

Revelation 3:10 because thou has kept the world of my patience, I will keep thee from the hour of temptation, which is come upon all the world to try them that dwell upon he earth

2 Peter 2:9 the Lord knows how to deliver the godly out of temptations, and to reserve the unjust unto the day of judgment to be punished

Ephesians 6:11 put on the whole armor of God, that ye may be able to stand against the wiles of the devil

Ephesians 6:12 For we wrestle not against flesh and blood, but against principalities, against rulers the darkness of this world, against spiritual wickedness in high places

Ephesians 6:13 wherefore take unto you the

whole armor of God that ye may be able to withstand in the evil day, and having done all to stand

Ephesians 6:14 Stand therefore, having your loins girt about with truth, having the breastplate of righteousness

Ephesians 6:15 and your feet shod with the preparation of the gospel of peace

Ephesians 6:16 and above all taking the shield of faith, wherewith ye shall be able to quench the fiery darts of the wicked

Ephesians 6:17 and take the helmet of salvation, and the sword of the Spirit, which is the word of God

Ephesians 6:18 praying always with all prayer and supplication in the Spirit and watching thereunto with all perseverance and supplication for all saints

Ephesians 6:19 And for me, that utterance my be given unto me, that I may open my mouth boldly, to make known the mystery of the gospel

2 Corinthians 2:15 he that is spiritual judges all things, yet he himself is judged of no man

Matthew 10:22 he that endures till the end shall be saved

1 Corinthians 10:13 There has no temptation taken you but such as is common to man: but God is faithful who will not suffer you to be tempted

above all that which ye are able; but will with the temptation also make a way to escape, that ye may be able to bear it

1 Corinthians 15:57 but thanks be to God, which gives us the victory through our Lord Jesus Christ

1 Corinthians 15:58 therefore, my beloved brethren, be ye steadfast, unmovable, always abounding, in the work of the Lord, forasmuch as ye know that your labor is not in vain in the Lord

Mark 13:13 ye shall be hated of all men for my name's sake; but he that shall endure until the end, the same shall be saved

Matthew 6:13 and lead us not into temptation but deliver us from evil

1 John 2:14 I have written unto you, fathers, because you have known him that is from the beginning. I have written unto you, young men, because ye are strong, and the word of God abides in you, and ye have overcome the wicked one

Luke 10:15 And thou Capernaum, are exalted to heaven, shall be thrust down to hell

Luke 12:36 and ye yourselves like unto men that wait for their lord, when he will return from the wedding; that when he comes and knocks, they may open unto him immediately

Luke 21:33 Heaven and earth shall pass away, but my words shall not pass away

Hebrews 7:21 the Lord swear and will not

repent

Luke 21:34 take heed to yourselves, lest ye be overcharged with surfeiting and drunkenness, and cares of this life, so that that day come upon you unawares

Luke 21:35 For as a snare shall it come upon them that dwell on the face of the whole earth

Luke 21:36 Watch ye therefore, and pray always, that ye may be able accounted worthy to escape all these things that shall come to pass, and to stand before the Son of man

Romans 5:9 much more then, being now justified by his blood, we shall be saved from wrath through him

1 Thessalonians 5:8 but let us, who are of the day, be sober, putting on the breastplate of faith, and love; and for an helmet, the hope of salvation

Revelation 20:4 …souls of them beheaded for the witness of Jesus, and for the word of God, which had not worshipped the beast and his image, neither had his mark in their foreheads, or in their hands, reigned with Christ for a thousand years.

OF NOTE: reject the beast's worship, and his image, or his mark in your foreheads, or in your hands, and you will go to heaven to be with Christ, forever.

Chapter Twenty-Three
God's Rapture Warning

But the righteousness which is of faith speaks on the wise, say not in thine heart, who shall ascend into heaven? (that is, to bring down Christ from the dead) Romans 10:6

Or, who shall descend from the deep? (that is, to bring up Christ again from the dead)

Romans 10:7

John 10:1 verily, verily I say unto you, he that enter not by the door into the sheepfold, but climb up some other way, the same is a thief and a robber

John 10:2 but he that enters in by the door is sheep of the shepherd

2 Thessalonians 2:11 for this cause, God shall send strong delusions

1 Timothy 4:1 now the spirit speaks expressly, that in latter times, some shall depart from the faith, giving heed to seducing spirits, and doctrines of devils

Romans 10:6 But the righteous, which is of faith, speaks on the wise, Say not in thine heart, who shall ascend into heaven? (that is, to bring Christ down from above)

Romans 10:7 Or, who shall descend from the deep? (that is, to bring up Christ again from the dead)

Leviticus 10:1 And Nadab, and Abhiu, the sons of Aaron, took either of them his censer, and put fire therein, and put incense thereon, and offered strange fire before the Lord, which he commanded them on

Leviticus 10:2 And there went out fire from the Lord, and devoured them, and they died before the Lord

Leviticus 20:6 And the soul that turn after such as have familiar spirits, and after wizards, to go a whoring after them I will even my face against that soul, and will cut him off from among his people

Deuteronomy 4:21 (For the Lord thy God is a merciful God) he will not forsake thee, neither destroy thee, nor forget the covenant of thy Father, which he swear unto them

Jeremiah 30:7 Alas! For that day is great that so that none is like it! It is even the time of Jacob's trouble; but he shall be saved out of it

Colossians 2:8 beware lest any man spoil you through philosophy vain deceit, after the tradition of men, after the rudiments of the world and not of Christ

1 John 4:1 Beloved, believe not every spirit, but try the spirits whether they are of God: because

many false prophets are gone out into the world

2 Thessalonians 2:9 …..we preach unto you the gospel of God

Isaiah 14:13 For thou has said in thine heart, I will ascend into heaven, I will exalt my throne above the thrones of God: I will also sit upon the mount of the congregation, in the sides of the north

Isaiah 14:14 I will ascend above the heights of the clouds; I will be like the most High

Isaiah 14:15 Yet thou shall be brought down to hell to the sides of the pit

Ezekiel 14:9 and if the prophet he deceived, when he has spoken a thing, I the Lord have deceived the prophet, and I will stretch out my hand upon him, and will destroy him from among the midst of my people

Ezekiel 14:10 And they shall bear the punishment of their iniquity: the punishment of the prophet shall be even as the punishment of him that seek unto him

Ezekiel 26:20 when I shall bring thee down with them that descend into the pit, with the people of old time, with the people of old time, and shall set thee in the low parts of the earth, in places desolate of old, and with them that go down to the pit, that thou be not inhabited; I shall set glory in the land of the living

Obadiah 1:4 Though thou exalt thyself, as the

eagle, and thou set thy nest among the stars, thence, will I bring thee down, said the Lord

Luke 10:15 And thou Capernaum are exalted to heaven shall be thrust down to hell

Hebrews 7:21 the Lord swear and will not repent

Luke 14:11 For whosoever exalts himself shall be abased; and he that humbles himself shall be exalted

Luke 16:15 …. For that which is highly esteemed among men is abomination to the sight of God

Matthew 3:7 but when he saw many of the Pharisees and Sadducees come to his baptism, he said unto them, O generation of vipers, who has warned you to flee from the wrath to come!

Matthew 12:34 O generation of vipers, how can ye, being evil, speak good things, for out of the abundance of the heart the mouth speaks

Matthew 23:37 O Jerusalem, O Jerusalem, thou that killed the prophets, and stone them which are sent unto thee, how often would I have gathered thy children, even as a hen gathers her chickens, under her wings, and ye would not

Matthew 11:23 and thou Capernaum which are exalted unto heaven, shall be brought down to hell: for if the mighty works which, which have been done in thee, had been done in Sodom, it would have remained until this day

Matthew 24:5 for many shall come in my name, saying, I am Christ, and shall deceive many

Ephesians 5:11 and have no fellowship with the unfruitful works of darkness, But rather reprove them

Ephesians 5:17 where be ye not unwise, but understanding, what the will of the Lord is

Hebrews 13:9 be not carried about with strange doctrines, diverse and strange doctrines

1 Corinthians 15:33 be not deceived, evil communications corrupt good manners

2 Corinthians 2:7 and lest I should be e exalted above measure through the abundance of revelations, there was given to me a thorn in the flesh, the messenger of Satan to buffet me, lest I should be exalted above measure

John 14:6 No man comes unto the Father, but by me.

2 Corinthians 11:13 For such are false prophets, deceitful workers, transforming themselves into apostles of light

2 Peter 2:1 But there were false prophets among the people, even as there shall be false teachers among you, who privily shall bring in damnable heresies, even denying the Lord that bought them, to bring upon themselves swift destruction

2 Peter 2:3 and through covetousness make merchandise of you: whose judgment now of a long

time lingers not and their damnation slumbers not

2 Peter 2:4 for God spared not the angels that sinned, but cast them down to hell, and delivered them to chains of darkness to be reserved unto judgment

Such heresy is not harmless, and God delivers a strong warning against such false beliefs, teachings, and practices.

Rapture beliefs, and teachings, is not only false, and fails on it's premise, but is malicious, delusional, and dangerous doctrine. If you want to continue and believe in such a doctrine, just remember, that God will not hold you blameless, but responsible. If, however, you want to discontinue the practice, just pray, and ask God to forgive you, of your sins. If not, be prepared to face God's wrath for this reckless behavior, and face separation from Him, altogether, and forever.

Saints should abandon the concept, notion, and false hope of a "rapture." You cannot avoid the coming great tribulation like that. Jesus Christ will not prey on unsuspecting, individuals, like an eagle or hawk, and forcibly carry them off to the wild -blue-yonder.

There will be no "sudden", "disappearing acts," to disrupt anyone, and "suddenly," "catching away," leaving their families, and employers, wondering where they are, without any warning.

There is also this mistaken notion, there aren't any false prophets, when in fact, scripture says, 'many' are gone out into the world. And that, 'many' more are deceived because of them. They come to you with lying signs and wonders to make merchandise of you.

Chapter Twenty-Four
Facts of the Case

If I were in a court of law, I would ask the judge for summary judgment, for 'A Case In Point,' against the "rapture." Why? because, Revelation 3:2 leads into scriptures like 1 Thessalonians 4:13-17

1 Thessalonians 4:13-17, and 1 Corinthians 15:51-52 cannot be taken at face value.

Christians have to prepare their hearts to meet God first, before they are ready to die. The old prophets, Enoch and Elijah, were not taken by force, as the "rapture," believers would have us to believe.

"snatching away," "catching away," "taken away,"

"carrying off," "seizure," "kidnapping," "rape," are all word origins for the term rapture.

These verbs can be considered criminal acts.

God will never force someone off the earth, stalked, or attacked, to be in heaven, if they are not ready to meet God, in the first place. The conditions must be right order or aligned.

"Rapture," is an antonym for misery, and synonym for ecstasy.

Misery and ecstasy should not be in Christian

theology, beliefs, or practices.

Rapture, the carrying of a person to another place or sphere of existence, or mental transport. This was first into circulation in the year 1600.

No one ascended with Jesus, as he ascended into heaven.

Jesus did not take apostles, the thief to his right, on the cross, prophets, and ascend into heaven with them.

No one has ever ascended, or received, into heaven, apart from Jesus Christ.

Jesus Christ was carried into heaven by his angels,

Jesus' angels, were already in heaven, and therefore, from heaven, as was Jesus Christ.

"Caught up," is not a word origin for the term "rapture." Rapture is a criminal act. "Caught up," is not.

Jesus never said, anyone would be "caught up," when he returns, the second time. Rapture, means, when you are forced into something, unwillingly.

John 13:26 wither I go, thou cannot follow me now, but thou shall follow me afterwards

John 21:23

A Case in Point

See, if you will notice, in these, "end times," the evangelicals, and leaders of the evangelicals, control a lot of political weight, and clout.

The Evangelicals have been openly supporting, and espousing politicians, whom they deem to support their ideas, or agendas, no matter the background, or motivation, of the individual in question.

Not to mention, many of their leaders are false prophets. Jeremiah 23:16 do not hearken to them.

This could very well end up being deception.

Through deception, the antichrist will soon come to power, if he isn't already.

A Case In Point: 60% to 80% of evangelicals, voted in huge numbers this past election to support one particular candidate.

Not Trump, nor, Michael Wolf, but Daniel 11:44 'fire and fury.'

The Evangelicals will push for a leader, they seem to think, mirrors their way of life, both politically and spiritually. He will exceed expectations and more, through his craftiness and deceivability.

VI

Evangelicals will soon find themselves at odds with the antichrist.

This antichrist will demand they take his mark, in their foreheads, or in their hands, and to worship his image, after he has deceived them into voting him into world dominance.

Of course, the Saints will resist this, and realize, they have made a huge, unforgivable, mistake for trusting this man. They will try once more to reason, or bargain with this leader, since they won't be able to buy, nor sell. But this effort will be too late, and futile.

The antichrist will kill them in huge numbers, by beheading them, Daniel 7:21, Revelation 12:17, 13:7

Revelation 12:7 there was war in heaven: Michael and his angels fought against the dragon, and the dragon fought and his angels

Who is able to make war with the beast? Revelation 13:4

John The Baptist was beheaded at Herod's behest.

God will turn the Saints, and Jews over to the antichrist, during the coming great tribulation period.

Revelation 13:7... all nations and kindred.

As was Job turned over to Satan, to do what he will, but without killing him, Job 16:11

Saints, Jews, the wicked, and non-Christians, Protestants, Muslims, Catholics, will be on an even playing field, during the great tribulation period.

Jere.23:11 for both the prophet and priest are profane; yea, in mine house have I found their wickedness, says the Lord

VII

Revelation 20:4 makes no specifications between either, Christian, or non-Christian, or for any length of time, they were either one.

Not to mention, you can go to hell, believing and trusting in a false doctrine, like the "rapture."

So, what is the point in discussing a "rapture?"

As the saying goes, "you can't get there from here."

Or rather, "rapture nuts are hard to crack."

Jeremiah 23:16 …the prophets fill you with false hopes.

The Belief in a so-called rapture is idolatry.

God will send a 'strong delusion,' if you continue to do otherwise, 2 Thessalonians 2:11

After the Evangelicals have elected the man they want in office, God will turn on them, as did, Saul, when he was made king of Israel. Israel wanted a king. God told Samuel to give them what they wanted, 1 Samuel 8:1-20.

After this, the Saints and non-Christians, during the great tribulation will be tried upon the earth, Revelation 3:10

After the Saints reject the antichrist's mark and his image, things will turn for the worse. Buying or selling will become an impossibility for them. Revelation 13:17

The only way out for the Saints, is to die in Christ. Revelation 14:13, and 7:14

If the Saints are still alive, they will be beheaded. Revelation 11:18, and 18:24

Among those 'left behind,' will be those in the second resurrection, and not the non-Christians, or "new-Christians," during the great tribulation period.

VIII

The Saints' voting bloc, will someday upend them.

And for all this, some Evangelicals have fooled themselves into believing, that in spite of their political missteps, that God will reward them with a "catching away," or "caught up," adventure.

They call this logic, delusional, and unrealistic.

Jesus Christ never preached or taught such an event. If that were true, he never would have warned you in Matthew about the fate of the Saints, Matthew 24:9

Matthew 27:52 and the graves were opened, and the many bodies of the Saints arose

Herein is the first resurrection. The ones, of whom, that are not saints, are in the second resurrection,

Revelation 20:4, 20:6, and 21:8, you are eternally separated from God in these verses. you can avoid the second resurrection, but not the first.

All aspects of a "rapture," are completely false, albeit a "pre-trib," "mid-trib," or "post-trib."

You cannot ascend into heaven, where God is, in the flesh. Read Romans 1. Romans 8:8 says, they that are in the flesh cannot please God.

The second resurrected dead will not see God in the air. The first resurrection, will Christ bring with him, not meet him.

John 6:63 it is the spirit that quickens: the flesh profits nothing…….

IX

So then, the spirit meets God in the air, and not the flesh, as a "rapture," would have you to believe.

So, I will ask you again, what is the point of a "rapture?" There is no validity. In fact, the term itself, should be outlawed. Let Go!

Only Jesus Christ has the authority to tell you about ascension into heaven, not Paul, or any other of the prophets, and apostles.

Christ's second coming is not a "rapture."

Jesus Christ forbids the talk of thoughts of such an event and is totally against the practice.

In this book, you will read that 1 Thessalonians 4:13-17, 1 Corinthians 15-51, and 1 Corinthians 15:52 have all been taken out of context, and at face value.

When you have scriptures like Revelation 3:2 to contend with. …. remain and ready to die…..

Not to mention, you won't see God and live. People that hold to a "rapture," hope to see God in the flesh.

Won't happen, ever. Exodus 33:20, John 1:18

Which is why God won't give credence or even dignify the terms, in the Holy Bible.

The same could be said of the Trinity, but, that's a whole other subject for this book, at this point and time.

The ideas for this book come from reading blogs and postings about the "rapture," on social media.

Let's face it, you will have to admit, the Saints are in the book of Revelation, and book of Daniel, front and center.

X

Self-appointed, assembly men, cunning, deceitful, selfish, thoughtless, self-absorbed, self-justifiable, smug, and contented, self-righteous, indifferent, untrustworthy, self-serving, exalted, thus, what is worse, therefore are imperfect before the eyes of God, aka, Evangelicals. Revelations 3:2. I have not found thy works perfect before God

Luke 14:11 For whosoever exalts himself, shall be abased: for he that humbles himself shall be exalted

Sanctified doesn't mean justified.

Sanctification doesn't mean justification, either.

The Evangelicals are the equivalent of the modern-day Pharisees, Sadducees, and Chief Priests.

Luke 18:11-12, could very well be the prayer of an Evangelical, as well. The Pharisee stood up and prayed thus with himself, God I thank thee, I am not as other men are, extortioners, unjust, adulterers, or even as this publican. 18:12, I fast twice in the week, I give tithes of all that I possess.

Acknowledgments

I wish to thank librarians, Karen Harrison, and Linda Warhurst, of the Mississippi County Library System, Keiser branch, located in Keiser, Arkansas., for their help and assistance, for research, and to provide additional information for this book.

The Keiser City Hall, MS. Nola Fincher, City Treasurer, MS. Nancy Coley, Water and City Clerk, and, Mayor Sandra Smith, for their enthusiasm and support.

Information and research for the completion of this book were gleaned from the following and social media sites:

   bible hub.com
   Hendrickson Publishing Marketing, LLC
   King James Concordance.com
   Dictionary.com
   Miriam-Webster.com
   Thomas Nelson Inc.,
Wikipedia, the free dictionary.com

The author of this book would like to thank each of

the following for their long-time friendship, and best wishes:

Hugh and Donna Adams
Billy and Peggy Allen
Mildred Allison
Eloise and James Anderson
Archie and Sherry Brannon
Arthur Brown
Cookie Cook
Travis W Cunningham
Shanijha Davis
Nathan and Amiee Dunman
Paul English
Rosemary Fair
Pauline "Polly" Faircloth
Juanita Frazier
Eddie and Linda Gardner
Danny and June Graham
Donald R. and Anita Hale
Tonya Marie Hooks
Melody Jarrett
Freddie Bee Kimbrough
Jamie Kimbrough
Linda Kirk
Curtis and Shonna Knighten
Jessie Knighten
William D and Kathryn Lambert

Harvey and Dorothy Lancaster
Skeeter Langston
Jerry Sue and Billy Larue
Daniel Lewellen
Ronald Martin
Vicky Morgan
Thelma Staples Newsome
Barbara Perkins
Cheryl Puckett
Dorothy Puckett
Mikala Razor
Harold and Nancy Senter
Travis and Edra Senter
Heather Sharp
Earnestine Seals Slie
Zed Thompson
Robert

Index

Aaron, 125,138, 139
abased, 60
abides, 58,136
Abihu, 138
Abiram, 125
able, 25,62,65,66,67,69,70,81, 102,107, 130,134,135,136
abominable, 45,128
abomination, 141
abounding, 136
above,   50,Jesus is from,62, that you are,12,54,62,102,122, 135, 139
Abraham, 81,93,97,104,106, 107,120
abroad, 63,93
absent, 107,109
abundance, 81,142
abundantly, 7
acceptable, 63, 64
accepting, 22
accomplish, 133
account, 26,46,96,114,115
accounted, 136, 137
actions, 1, 71
Acts 1:3, 49
Acts 1:9, 49
Acts 1:11, 49
Acts 1:10, 32

Acts 1:11, 33,91
Acts 1:12, 91
Acts 2:19-21, 86
Acts 2:27, 98
Acts 2:29, 94,112
Acts 2:34, 50,94, 112
Acts 2:35, 50, 94
Acts 3:20-21, 86
Acts 2:38, 38
Acts 3:20-21, 29
Acts 4:1, 42
Acts 4:2, 42
Acts 8:39, 34
Acts 8:40, 34
Acts 10:25-26, 52
Acts 10:42, 46, 91
Acts 14:15, 52
Acts 14:22, 67
Acts 24:15, 18,42, 94
Acts 28:6, 52
Adam, 23, 94, 95, 96
adultery, 67
advantage, 24
affirmities, 46
afflicted, 63, 84
afraid, 105
after, 59, 67,83,87
afterwards, 26,59follow me,145

African, 16
against, 69,72,73,74,to speak words 78,90,103,125,135,139
Ahab, 97
air, 30,47,114,115
alive, 23,38,43,47,49,95, 115,120, 96,126
allow, 18,94
already,   66,102
altars, 97,108
ancient, 10, 54, 74, 85,116
alarm, 69,70
Alas! 67,69,139
Alleluia, 80
aligned, 144
Almighty, 68,69,79,80
alone, 97,99
altar, 78, 97,108
always, 41,97,135praying
Amos 5:19, 127
Amos 9:2,   2
angels, 17,30,33,52,53,55,56, 61,63,64,65,73,78,79,84,87,97,96,97,104,107,108,109,110,115 143,145
anger, 28, 68,69,133
anguish, 66,67,76
antichrist, 9,14,
anyone, 57is in Christ,63
apparel, 33

appear, 12,17, 25,39? 51, 63,
false67prophets,67,87,90,91,96, 110, 111,126
appeared, 4,49,to Simon, 53,113
appearing, 42,91,92,95,110, 114
appertain, 125
appertained, 125,126
apex, 3
appoint, 31,88,89
appointed, 44, 46,59, 61,96
apostles, 63,127,142,145
archangel, 43,45,92,114,115
arise, 41,42
ark, 119
armies, 90, 91
army, 91
armor, 134
arose, 42, 88
Artaxerxes, 10
ascend, 1, 2, 12, 50, 79, 138,139,140
ascending, 50
ascended, 6, 9,30,37,50,51,54,94,112,131, 132,145
ashamed, 97,
aside, 104
asleep, 22,42,90,91,108,115
assembly, 107
asunder, 5,31,88,125
author, 117
authority, 23

avoid, 51,62,117
awake, 41,44,69,85,114
awakening,71
away, 58 old things passed,60heaven and   earth, 63,75,78wipe away,85
102
aware, 31,88,89
Azotus, 34

Babel, 1
Babylon, 2, 30
banished, 94
Baptist, 44
Baptist John The 50,107,113
baptisms, 35,44
baptized, 22,37,93,94,97
bear, 62,90,102,127,128,130
beast, 8,15,16,70,71,73,74,76,
78,79,80,82,83,90,118,120,124 137
bed, 19,67,85,89,111
before, 12,13,31,33,43,46,70,75,77,93,102,108,110,113,115, 131
began, 29,81,83,92
beggar, 97,101,107
beginning, 64,67,96,97,136
begotten, 62,96,97,101,105
behalf, 64,68,70,75,99

behavior, 25
beheaded, 15,16,63,65,70,74, 76,79, 80, 82,113,118,124,137
behind, 50
beheld, 32,73,78
behold, 32,33,104,105
behoved, 66
Belial, 120
beliefs, 15, 25
believe, 18,20,24.30,42,58,62, 64,68,70,72,74,75,78,87,90,91,94,95,99,105,106,111, 123,139
belong, 117
beloved, 25,71, 78,82,83,139
beneath,   82, 86,36, 48,82
beseech, 117
besought, 123
better, 22,61,65,111
betwixt, 111
beware, 139
beyond, 10
Bible, 15
biblical, 116,117,124
bite, 127
blaspheme, 15,103
blasphemed, 13,14,15,29,31,96
blasphemy, 14,15, 103
bless, 95, 96,99,100

blessed, 21,41,88,92
blind, 69
blood,12,13,14,16,29,65,66,6872,73,74,76,77,78,80,2,86,90, 113,118,119,124, 137
bodies,8,40,70,88,104,105,
body,10,23,25,33,37,44,45,93,97,102,104,105,106,107,109, 112,116,117, 122,
boils, 52
boldly, 135
boldness, 67,70,93,97
bond, 44,46
bondage, 92,96
book, 14,69,79,92,103,107
born, 4,37,57,35,46,58,97,101,102 107
borne, 51,98,105
bosom, 62,93,97,98,100,101, 105,107
both, 4, 40,66,71,91, 94,112
bottomless pit, 76,79,83
bought, 19, 127
bound, 111
bow, 133
bowed, 121
brass, 15
bread, 97,133
breadth, 83
breastplate, 127, 129,135,137
breath,16,120

brethren,16,41,57,58,63,94, 103,108,112,114,117,156,
bridegroom, 86, 88
brimstone, 16,18,19,45,80,83, 122, 128
bring, 7,12,25,42,87,103,116,131,132
bringing, 78,120
brother, 16, 37,94,111,113
brought, 1, 2,10,130,132,140
bud, 133
buffed, 117
buffet, 123
build, 10,16,17
buried, 48,94,97,101,107,112
burn, 122,128
burned, 25, 98
burnt, 98,99,104
burned, 24,99,104
bush, 98,99,104
bury, 72
buy, 73

Caesarea, 34
cakes, 28
call, 86
called, 80
camp, 16,83
cannot, 25,32,37,sin,46,51,see my
face,54,62,63,112,122,133,98

Capernaum, 2,136,141
captains, 42,61,65
captive, 81,84,86,102
carcasses, 38,87
cares, 60
carried, 51,53,97,107,142
cast, 9,20,56,67,73,81,20,106
cattle, 119,120
caught, 32,33,34,45,54,86
caught away, 33
caught up, 54,90.115,122
cause, 27.29.,77,138
cave, 97
Cease, 29
censer, 79,108,124,139
certain, 9,17,41,44,57,74
chains, 73,143
chambers, 20
change, 24,74
changed, 33,42,44,45,50,62,89,92,110, 115
charge, 45,73,87,91,92,95,110
charger, 113
chariot, 4
cheer, 67
chickens, 98,141
chief, 65
child , 54

children, 17,
32,56,69,77,82,98,101,106,117125,129,141,97
choose, 112,124
Christ,12,16,20,21,22,25,34,4143,44,45,46,50,58,60,61,
63,64,65,66,70,76,71,75,76,81,84,92,93,95,96,97,99,111,
112,118, 122,123,124,130,137,138,81,
82,93,103,139,141, 142
Christ Jesus, 23,68
Christian, 34,43.44,144
church, 32, 70, 107,115,
Churches of saints, 117
Church of God, 73
cities, 30,34,70,122
city, 30,83,108
clave, 125
clean, 73,87,90
cleave, 87
climb, 2,138
closed, 126
clothed, 87,90,118
clothes, 111
clothing, 126
clouds,1,2,4,5,10,12,19,25,30,32,47,54,55,67,85,87,89,1
15, 118, 119,140, 82,83,86
coast, 99
cock, 60
colored, 15
Colossians 1:13, 3, 58

Colossians 1:15, 105
Colossians 2:8, 139
come, 62,67,69,74,88,91,92, 102
comfort, 46,47,70,80,84
coming, 2,55, 67,83,86,87,89,115,119
command, 2
commanded, 10,83,139
commandments, 8,18,73,95
commit, 14,37,38,67
committed, 36,84
common, 102
communications, 142
commuting, 120
company, 124,125
compared, 10, 106
compassed, 16,80,83
concerning, 25,40,74,77,82,103,108,114
concord, 126
condemn, 66
condemned ,121
conditions, 144
confess, 42
confident, 107,109,
confirm, 29
confusion, 28,117
congregation,124,125,126, 140
conscience, 117
considers, 102

considering, 129
consume, 74
consumed, 104,105,121,125,126
contain, 10
contempt, 48,69,82,86,114
contrary, 97,117
controversy, 51
conversation, 24,121
1 Corinthians 6:14,21, 39
1 Corinthians 5:10, 111
1 Corinthians 5:18, 42
1 Corinthians 6:14, 41
1 Corinthians 10:13, 60, 61,130
Colossians 3:4, 25
1 Corinthians 12:2-5, 46
1 Corinthians 14:33, 117
1 Corinthians 15:13-19, 22
1 Corinthians 15:18, 43
1 Corinthians 15:21-31, 23
1 Corinthians 15:22, 96, 111
1 Corinthians 15:26-27, 95
1 Corinthians 14:32, 24
1 Corinthians 15:32, 24
1 Corinthians 15:33, 142
1 Corinthians 15:42, 39
1 Corinthians 15:51, 33,45
1 Corinthians 15:52, 24,33,42,44,95,96,110,132
1 Corinthians 15:51-52, 45

1 Corinthians 15:55, 129
1 Corinthians 15:57, 129,135
2 Corinthians 2:7, 142
2 Corinthians 11:13, 142
2 Corinthians 12:1-8, 22
2 Corinthians 4:10, 96
2 Corinthians 5:17,61, 63
2 Corinthians 6:15, 126
2 Corinthians 7:4, 10, 84
1 Corinthians 10:13, 61
1 Corinthians 10:32, 73
2Corinthians 7:4, 84
2 Corinthians11:14, 64
2 Corinthians 11:13, 63
2 Corinthians 12:2-5, 33,45,52
2 Corinthians 12:3-4, 34
2 Corinthians 12:4, 34
Cornelius, 52
corruptible, 42
corrupt, 119, 142
corrupted, 119
corruption, 41, 98, 112
count, 25
country,9,20,44,56,83,106
covenant,29,68,69,72,139
covets, 2
covetousness,2, 126, 142
crack, 126

created, 8
creature, 7,58,98,103,105,108
creed,103
creeping, 120
creeps, 120
criminal, 145
crow, 60
crown, 97,102,103,134
crucified, 38,107,112
cruel, 69
cry, 120,125,126
cut, 1,31,89,139

daily, 23,71,74
damnable,13,127,142
damnation,20,39,42,121,127, 142
dangerous, 143
Daniel 7:13-14, 85
Daniel, 7:18,14, 71
Daniel 7:21-22,13, 71
Daniel 7:25-27, 71
Daniel 8:13, 71
Daniel 9:5, 36
Daniel 9:27, 29
Daniel 12:2,85, 114
darkened,12,19,64,67,87,101

darkness,
4,20,56,58,67,69,73,86,88,106,123,127,129,133,
134,135,142,143
darts,127,135
Dathan, 125
David, 50, 94,112
day,4,10,16,19,25,30,44,54, 60,65,66,67,68,69,71,
100,102,110,111,78,84,85,86,88,89,94,121,27,134,139
dead,12,18,20,21,22,23,24,27,33,38,39,42,43,44,45,46,53,58,66,72,87,88,90,91,92,93,94,95,96,111,104,112,113,
114,115, 130, 138,139
deal,   39
debacle, 1
depart, 11,111,123
departing, 36
dear, 4, 58
death, 4,23,36,37,38,44,45,48, 57,58,59,60,61,65,71,
72,74,93,94,95,96,97,106,112,122,124,128,129,134
deceit, 131,139
deceitful, 63,134,142
deceive, 37,63,75,77,83,93,126
deceived, 58,60,63,72,74,80,84,83,112,
117,121,130,132,133,140,142
declared,62,83,105
decree, 10
deeds,15,67,106,112
deep?,12,27,130,138
deeper, 4

defiled, 79,118,123
deliver, 62,63,65,70,73,81,40,84,93, 100,102,127,134
deliverance, 22
delivered,2,4,9,65,69,70,73,80121,134,143
delusion, 27,28,77,130,138
delusional, 27,143
deny, 17,41,44,59
denying, 127,142
depart, 11,17,105,111,30
departing, 84
descend,12,27,45,50,109,115,130, 131, 132,138,139
descended, 9,45,54
descending, 50
descent, 91
dessert,   20
desire, 71, 111,
desired, 106,113
desolate,66,69,88,132,140
desolation,67,74,128
destroy,68,69,71,85,96,105,
112, 118,119,120,121
14,115,131
destroyed,19,23,38,85,95,106
112,117
destruction,57,69,122,127,128134,142
Deuteronomy 4:12, 90, 105,111
Deuteronomy 4:21, 131
Deuteronomy 4:30-31, 68

Deuteronomy 10:14, 10
Deuteronomy 29:29, 117
devil,56,83,84,89,93,96,102,127,130,135
devils, 11,15,17,138
devise, 94
devoured,16,70,83,131,139
die,13,23,24,25,33,45,46,47,5156,57,58,59,61,62,63,71, 76,84,90,94,95,96,110
died,4,17,38,43,87,90,95,97, 107,112,114,119,120,131,139
dig, 2
digged, 97
diligent, 61
diligently,10
dipped, 90
divided, 30, 86
divides, 7, 57
dividing, 74
divisions, 117
disciple, 51,53,58,63,88,92,94
discontinue, 134
disobedient, 84,112
disobedience, 36,77,117,129
distress, 69,89
divers, 84,112,117
diverse, 142
divisions,111
doctrine,11,17,46,117,130,133

138
dogs,118
doing, 61,65
dominion,38,70,71,74,85,95
done, 30, it is39 good, or evil
door, 28,62,125,133,138
dot, 114
doubt, 69
doubtless, 122
dough, 28
down,1,2,73,119,130132,133, 134
dragon, 63,72,84
drank, 19
draw, 104
drink, 24,77
drowned,114,115
drunken, 13,80,118
drunkeness,58,59,60,129,137
dung, 2, 70
duped, 116,127
dust, 41,48,69,70,85,114
dwell, 59,64,67,78
diligent, 59
diverse,133
dwell,10,29,70,78,79,103,129
dying, 17

eagle, 87,140,143
ears, 117
earth,4,7,8,10,12,14,16,17,25,41,48,54?60,67,68,69,70,72,7880,85,86,89,90,98,101,103,107108,114,119,124125, 126,128, 133,134
earthquake, 30
eat, 14, 94
Ecclesiastes 7:15, 130
Ecclesiastes 8:14, 130
Ecclesiastes 9:5, 97
ecstasy, 144
eighth, 120
Elijah, 3,4,5,66,97,144
elect, 63,126
elders, 68,75,79
elements, 8, 25,
Elias, 113
Elisha, 6, 31
employers, 143
end,23,24,26,36,41,56,57,62, 74, 92, 102,103,125,135
endure, 62,102,135,136
enemies, 23, 30,
enemy, 95, 101
enlarge, 99
Enoch, 3,4,5,6,58,144
ensample, 121
enter, 57,62,65,138
entered,   36,74,94

envy, 117
Ephesians 4:10, 6
Ephesians 5:8, 129
Ephesians 5:11,142
Ephesians 5:17, 142
Ephesians 6:8, 46
Ephesus, 24
erect, 1
err, 18
error, 73
escape, 41,55,57,60,62,102,121,130, 136, 137
eschewed, 122
Esaias, 82
esteemed, 141
eternal, 37,46,95,112
eternally, 28
eunuch, 34
ever, 73, 83
everlasting, 41,48,69,71,85,114
evermore, 100
everyone, 38
evil,2,13,20,32,39,42,61,62,65,66,76,81,99,100,101,102, 121, 122,128, 129,130,132,136,141
exalt, 1,2,60,140
exalted, 2,8,60,12,123,136,141
142
exceeding, 31,70
exceedingly, 70, 84

excellency, 1, 2
executed, 133
exhort, 117
Exodus 3:2-6, 104
Exodus 33:20, 3,6,110
expectation, 96
expelled, 94
explanation, 35
expedient, 122
expressly, 17,138
eye,15,25,33,44,45,78,90,92, 97,105,107,110,115,119
Ezra, 35
Ezra 7:10,24,26,36,40,47,92, 110, 114
Ezekiel 14:9,117,140
Ezekiel 14:9-10, 140
Ezekiel 26:20, 140
Ezra 7:21, 106

face, 6, 7,51,60,105,121
132,137
faces, 28,54
fades, 133
failing, 89
faith,4,11,17,27,50,58,96,135,138,139
faithful,16,62,80,90,97,101, 102,134,136
Faithful, 16
fall, 12,55,67,82,?87,127,128

fallen, 1, 22,52
fame, 112
familiar, 139
false, 22,63,83,126,127,128
140,142,143
fashioned, 24
fast, 57,61,90,102,103
Father,13,17,20,22,43,51,52,
59,60,62,71,79,87,100,101,105139,142
fathers, 28,68,81,93,102,104,128
fault, 119,123
favor, 39
feed, 54,78
fed, 97
fear, 10,30,89,96,127,128
fearful, 45,128
feared, 122
feet, 23,30,52,87,95,104,135
fell, 38
fellowship, 129,142
fenced, 69
fervent, 8, 25,
fervently, 58
few, 14
field, 8,19,20,31,55
fierce, 69
fierceness, 30
fell, 30,31,52

fiery, 77,135
fifth, 78
fifty, 97
figure, 95
fill, 9, 54
filled, 70,84,91
find, 58,62,63,71
fine, 90
filthy, 121
finish, 89
finished, 79
fire, 5,6,19,28,56,70,80
83,86,90,100,104,105,126
128,139
firmament, 4, 7,
first, 54,72,92,107,115
firstborn, 105
firstfruits, 22,79,118,123
flame, 90,104
fled, 30,54,126
flee, 36, 67,71,81,127,128,141
flesh, 48,52,53,70,72,91,95,105,112, 119,131,135,142
flood, 19,120
flower, 133
fly, 7,108
flying, 78
forcibly, 143
foes, 50, 94

follow, 26,58,59,79,105,118,123, 127,145
followers, 101
followed, 90
food, 119
foolish, 84,88,117
foot, 58,74,100,111
footstool, 50,94
forbid, 82
force, 96
forgotten, 97
forsake, 68,72,98,139
foreheads, 76,79,80,118,137
forever, 2,58,72,98,133
forget, 68,139
foreheads, 16,76.79,80,82,103,123,124, 134
forgive, 60
fornication, 14,15
found, 13,14,16,33,38,58,61,68,123, 128
foundation, 79, 103
fountains, 78
fought, 24,43,63,84
fourteen, 34,122
fortify, 2,
forty, 38
found, 16,53,72,80,118,124
fowl, 7,8,10, 72, 91, 108
free, 46
freed, 38, 95

freely, 94,112,
friends, 128
fruits, 81,112
full, 15
fulfilled, 83
furnace, 56

gain, 43,75,76,84,95
Galatians 1:4, 100
Galilee, 33,49
garden, 9
garment, 56
gate, 121
gather, 28,56,72,98,141
gathered, 17,56,57,87,90,94,98,102,125
gazing, 33
general, 107
Genesis 5:22-24, 4
Genesis 1:1-8, 4
Genesis 1:6-8, 5
Genesis 1:6, 7
Genesis 1:7, 7
Genesis 1:8, 7
Genesis 1:14, 7
Genesis 1:17, 7
Genesis 1:20, 7
Genesis 2:4, 8

Genesis 6:9, 119
Genesis 6:12-14, 119
Genesis 6:17, 119
Genesis 7:21, 119
Genesis 17:19, 121
Genesis 17:34, 121
Genesis 18:20, 120
Genesis 18:23, 120
Genesis 18:33, 120
Genesis 19:1, 120
Genesis 19:13, 121
Genesis 19:17, 121
Genesis 22:14, 64, 93
generations, 8,35,39,67,81, 119,141
Gentiles,52, 65,67,73,76,81,82
gift,39,95,97,112
girt, 135
glass, 80
gloominess, 69
glorified, 98
glory,12,15,17,19,46,52,55,61,62,65,67,74,75,80,87,89,99, 106,122,140
glorying, 70
gnashing, 20,31,56,88,107
goats, 57
God, 4,5,7,9.10,13,15,18,28,29,30, 31,33,37,39,45,46,51,52,57,58,60,65,67,68,70,71,72,3,75,76, 77,78,79,80,81,82,90,92,94,95,

99,100,101,102,104,105,106,
108,110,112,115,117,121,122,
128,131,132,135,140,143,144
gods, 28, 52
Godliness, 52
godly, 64,68,75,84,102
gold, 15, 70
golden, 78, 108
Gomorrah, 120, 121
good,8,20,39,46,55,64,67,101,111, 121
goods, 9, 125
goodly, 8
gospel, 92, 135, 140
grace, 96,119
granted,100
grass, 133
graves, 20, 93? 111, 130
great, 8,12,15,19,25,29,30,31,52,55,
66,67,68,70,76,78,80,87,89,92, 100,121,126,139
greater, 93
greatness, 74
greatly, 18
grain, 8, 9
grieve, 100
grieved, 38
grievous, 121
grinding, 19,31, 89
ground, 1, 94,104,121,125

guests, 56
guile, 38,66,119

habitation, 10
Habakkuk 20:9, 2,
hail, 15, 31
half, 30 ,87
Hallowed, 106
hand, 2,15,16,26,36,41,46,49,56,57, 65, 69, 70,74,76,81, 82,93,100,118,119,123,124,127
happened, 77
happens, 130
harm, 52
harps, 80
hated, 62,84,102
hateful, 84,117
hating, 84,117
harvest, 56
heap, 117
hear, 15,18,20,39,81,113,124
heard, 18,43,46,51,74,78,80,89,90, 105,108,112
hearken, 129
heart, 1,11,12,27,31,36,40,41,42,4,50 58,81,89,92,101?,102,110,114, 129,133,138,140
heat, 8,15,78,100
heathen, 129

heaven, 1,2,4,5,6,7,8,9,10,12,16,17,18,24,28,29,30,31,32,33? 34,37,41?43,45,46,49?50,51, 54,55,63,67,69,71,72,74,78,80,84,85,86,87,88,94,103,106,107108,119,122131,132 133,137,138, 145

Hebrews 2:9, 65, 96

Hebrews 2:14-15, 96

Hebrews 2:18, 66

Hebrews 6:2, 45

Hebrews 7:21, 141

Hebrews 9:27, 45, 96

Hebrews 11:5, 4

Hebrews 11:13, 96

Hebrews 11:35, 22

Hebrews 12:14, 105

Hebrews 13:9, 142

heed, 55

hen 98, 141,143

henceforth, 38,102

Hereafter,28,50

heavens, 1,2,8,12,25,27?28,45,47,50,67,90

heed, 55,17

heights, 2,9,140

helmet, 137

heresies, 142

Herod, 112,113

Herodias, 113

herself, 14
hell, 2,8,44,73,97,98,107,136,140, 141, 143
hid, 8,104
high, 2?,8,9,10,13,71Most,73,74,90
higher, 9
Himself, 49, alive 66suffered100,
115,
hold, 57
holiness, 105
holy,   21,29,41,104,124
holy city, 42
Holy Ghost, 94,97
Holy One, 98
honor, 80, 89
hope, 18,86,92,94,96,114
horn, 13, 73
horse, 91,123
horses, 90
hot, 117
hour, 13,20,23?31,55,57,61,70,77,8788,89,101
house, 2,10,107,125 houses
housetop, 19
howbeit, 52
howl, 69
humbles, 60
Hundred and forty four thousand, 79,118,123
hunger, 78
hurt, 101,103,134

hypocrisy, 117
hypocrites, 31,35,88

idols, 14,15
idolaters, 45,118,128
ignorant, 25,42,108,114
image, 16,70,76,80,82,105,118,124, 137
imagined, 1,
immediately, 12,28, 67,87,89,136
incense, 108,124,125,126
incorruptible, 33,44,58,92,110,115
incorruption, 41
indeed, 10,50,53,99
infallible, 47
infidel?, 126
infirmities, 122
iniquity, 36,56,84,140
inhabitant, 77,78
inhabited, 140
inherit, 83
instant, 117
instructed, 113
instruments, 38
invisible, 105
iron, 54,117
itching, 117
Isaiah 13:6, 69

Isaiah 13:9, 69
Isaiah 14:12-15, 1
Isaiah 14:13-15, 140
Isaiah 14:14, 2
Isaiah 14:15, 140
Isaiah 26:10, 39
Isaiah 26:14, 39
Isaiah 40:8, 133
Isaiah 45:23, 133
Isaiah 55:10, 133
Isaiah 55:11, 133
Isaiah 57:1, 129
island, 30
Israel, 11,24,26,36,40,47,82,99,100, 110,118,126
Isaac, 52,104,106
Jabez, 99
Jacob's, 66,68,69,106
jealousy, 70,82
Jeopardy, 23
Jeremiah 7:18-19,   28
Jeremiah 23:16, 129
Jeremiah 23:20, 133
Jeremiah 30:7, 68
Jeremiah 51:53, 2
Jerusalem, 65,86,87,98,108
Jesus Christ, 18,24,37,39,44,51,59,61,62,63,65,70,73,76,80,86,88,90.91,92,94,97,112,118,124

136, 137
Jews, 32, 64, 66, 73, 93
Jezebel, 14, 97
Job, 122
Job 1:1, 122
Job 1:12, 122
Job 3:26, 76
Job 11:8, 4
Job 16:11, 76
Job 19:26-27, 105
Job 20:6-7, 2
Job 39:27, 2
John The Baptist, 52, 113
1John 1:8, 37, 75
1John 1:10, 37, 75
1John 3:5, 37, 39, 75
1 John 3:9, 37
1 John 4:1, 128
1 John 4:12, 51
John 4:24, 13
1 John 5:16-17, 37
John 1:18, 105. 132
John 1:51, 50
John 4:12, 105
John 4:23-24, 13
John 5:21, 20
John 5:28-29, 20
John 5:29, 39

John 5:37, 51, 105
John 6:46, 5, 105
John 6:62-63, 53
John 3:13, 37, 131, 132
John 7:34, 58, 62
John 11:25-26, 58
John 8:21, 25, 62
John 8:23, 37
John 8:24, 62
John 8:26, 37
John 8:34, 33, 38
John 8:52-53, 93
John 13:13, 50
John 8:21, 51,62
John 8:23, 50
John 10:9, 62
John 11:25-26, 58
John 13:26, 26
John 13:33, 59
John 13:36-38 , 59
John 14:1-3, 32
John 14:2-3. 32, 107
John 14:6, 62, 142
John 14:16, 142
John 14:19, 62
John 16:10, 32, 59
John 16:16, 32
John 16:28, 51

John 16:33, 67, 75
John 17:4, 98
John 17:10, 98
John 17:15, 13,32, 128, 132
John 17:15-23, 99
John 19:26, 54, 62
John 19:26, 62
John 20:17-18, 51
John 20:20, 51
John 20:25, 51
John 21:14, 53
John 21:23-24, 51, 53
John 21:22-23, 58
John 21:23, 63, 93
John 24:26, 65
John 24:51, 53
journey, 86
joyful, 70, 83
judge, 27,44,45,46,86,90,91,102, 107,117,110,114,115
judged, 135
judges, 135
judgment, 11,24,26,36.40,44,46,47,59,61,72,73,74,80,82,84,92,96,98, 102,110,111,114,127,134,142
just, 18,42,65,80,86,94,1-7,130
justified, 52,137

keep, 13,32,61,70,73,99,100,101,103128
keeper, 100
kept, 29,61,70,77,101
kingdom 3,5,8,9,10,14,43,45,56,57,58,
60,62,70,71,73,74,75,81,106, 110,114
kill, 66,77,79,84
killed, 15,97,98,141
kindle, 28
kindred, 13,25,79,103,109
king, 56,80,90
1 Kings 8:27, 10
2 Kings 2:11, 3
2 Kings 2:11-12, 4
2 Kings, 2:16-17, 3
knead 28
knee, 133
knew, 34
knocks, 136
know, 6,34,46,55,62(s)84,88,100,134
known, 136
Korah, 124,125

labor, 43, 115, 128
lads, 100
LaHaye, Tim 116,127
laid, 92,113,125
Lake of Fire, 31,45,83,128

Lamb, 29,78,79,118,122
Lamps, 88,89
land, 69,70,80,120,122,140
languages, 85
last, 33,44,45,110,111,115
latter, 11,17,68,138
law,10,11,24,26,36,40,47,92, 106,110,114,117
lawful, 34,113,122
laying, 46
lays, 59,102
Lazarus, 107,111
lead, 78,100
learn, 79
learned, 117
less, 10
leave, 17,98
leaven, 9
leavened, 9
left,17,18,19,31,57,72,96,107, 115,120
lest, 121,125
Levi, 124
Leviticus 10:1-2, 139
Leviticus 20:6, 139
liar, 37,45, 128
lie, 27,28,77,117,118
life,7,19,20,22,25,30,32,37,39,42,48,59,60,69,79,85,95,96, 103,114,119,120,121,134,137
lifetime, 96

lifted, 96,107
lights,7,12,22,63,64,67,78, 88,129,142
lightings,30,88
like,52,66,68,69,86,136,140
likewise, 19
linen, 90
lingers, 127,142
lion, 127
little,32,59,60,61,62,65,83,101
125
live,6,38.43,51,54,68,95,105, 110,111,115,121,132
lived, 16,21,38,76,82,123
lives, 58,84,101,110,111
living, 18,78,84,96,140
Lo, 20, 79, 123
locusts, 101
loins, 135
look,24,31,61,88,90,91,108, 121
looked, 28,32,52,79,123
looking, 89,92
lose, 19
loose, 111
loosed, 83
long, 127,142
longsuffering, 25,117
Lord,6,8,10,18,21,23,24,25,26,28,36,40,42,43,45,46,48,
50,59,68,69,70,80,86,89,92,93,94,98,

100,102,104,105,106,110,114,
115,117,120,121,122,125,129
137,139,140,141
lose, 19
Lot, 19,20,121
loud, 78,92,108,111
love, 64,72,98,115,118,137
loved, 98
low, 140
lower, 54,60,61,65,96
Lucifer, 1,
Luke 3:7,39, 67
Luke 3:7-8, 81
Luke 9:7-9,113
Luke 9:19, 113
Luke,9:27,24,41,44,60
Luke 9:31, 39
Luke 13:21, 9
Luke 13:35, 60
Luke 14:11, 60
Luke 18:32-33, 65
Luke 19:37, 91
Luke 21:3, 60
Luke 21:33, 137
Luke 21:34-36, 137
Luke 21:35, 67
Luke 21:36,41, 70
Luke 23:34, 60

Luke 24:24, 53
lusts, 38,117
magnified, 97
majesty, 39
malice, 84,117
man, 12, 17,19,20,23,32,34,36 38,45,46,50,51,52,62,73,74,79.85,87,93,94,96,105,107,1 12, 120,122,125,127,129,130,132,133,142
manna, 94
manner, 24,33,49,65,86,142
manifest, 52
manifested, 37,39,75
mansions, 32,107
many, 32,42,63,69,84, 93,107,126,142
mark, 16,73,76,80,82,124
Mark 10:34, 66
Mark 12:22, 18
Mark 12:23-29, 18
Mark 13:13, 62,136
Mark 13:24, 19
Mark 13:26, 19
Mark 14:62, 88.119
Mark 16:19, 6, 88
Mark 110:33-34, 66
marry, 18
marriage, 9, 18,19
married, 19
martyrs, 14,80,118

marvel, 20, 64
marvelous, 80
Mary Magdalene, 51
master, 6,
Matthew 13:24, 8,19
Mark 13:26, 19
Matthew 3:7, 35,81,141
Matthew 6:13, 62,100,136
Matthew 7:15, 126
Matthew 7:28, 107
Matthew 11:23, 141
Matthew 12:34, 81,141
Matthew 13:25-26, 55
Matthew 13:31, 8,
Matthew 13:32-33, 55
Matthew 13:37-38, 55
Matthew 13:39-42, 56
Matthew 13:33, 8,
Matthew 13:44-45, 8,
Matthew 13:47, 9,
Matthew 13:49-50, 56
Matthew 14:2, 112
Matthew 14:3-4, 113
Matthew 14:8, 113
Matthew 16:27, 87
Matthew 16:28, 49, 56
Matthew 17:11, 6
Matthew 17:23, 66

Matthew 18:23, 9.
Matthew 21:43, 81
Matthew 22:2, 9,
Matthew 22:11, 56
Matthew 22:13, 56
Matthew 23:37, 98,141
Matthew 24:5,84,93,130,141
Matthew 24:11, 126
Matthew 24:21, 67
Matthew 24:24, 93,126
Matthew 24:29-31, 67
Matthew 24:29, 12
Matthew 24:29-30, 17
Matthew 24:26, 20
Matthew 24:29-30, 67
Matthew 24:30, 17
Matthew 24:31, 67
Matthew 24:50-51, 88
Matthew 25:1, 9,
Matthew 25:30, 20,56
Matthew 25:31-32, 17
Matthew 25:32, 17,57
Matthew 25:33, 57
Matthew 25:3-5, 88,89
Matthew 25:4-5, 88
Matthew 25:12-13, 88
Matthew 25:14, 9,
Matthew 25:30, 88

Matthew 26:41, 57
Matthew 24:27-30, 87
Matthew 24:36, 87
Matthew 27:52-53, 42
Matthew 27:52, 88
McDonald, Margaret, 116
meal, 9,
means , 101
meant, 121
meet, 47
melt, 25
measures, 9, 123,142,
meat, 8, 72
meet, 35,47,121
Melchisedec, 52
members, 38,112
memory, 39,97
men, 15, 89,69,20,23,25,31,33,44,46,49, 70,71,79,89,94,97,100,101,102105,111,112,125,129,130, 136
merchandise, 127,142
merchant, 8,
merciful, 68,102,139
mercy, 10
messenger, 123, 142
Messiahs, 63, 126
Methuselah, 4,
Michael, 69, 84

midst, 7, 78,104,108,118,128
mighty, 30, 92,141
mill,   31
minds, 52, 64
mingled, 80,129
miserable,   22
mocked, 65
moment, 33,44,45,92,110,115
moon,`12, 73,86,89,100
morning!, 1, 2,
mortal, 38
mortify, 112
Moses, 80,94,104,125
Most High, 14,71,73,74
mother, 54,62,113,
motions, 112
mount, 1,86, 87
mourn, 12, 17, 67
mountain, 2, 30,52,87,121
mouth, 29,38,66,81,86,119,123,125, 129
moved, 119
moving, 7,
multitude, 81,92
murderers, 15, 45,118
murmur, 125, 129
mustard, 8, 9,
myself, 32,45,52,89,133
mystery, 33,45,52,110,135

Nadab, 139
name's, 15,62,63,79,84,102,
name, 15,63,73,79,80,93,97,103,108,130
Nations!, 1, 13,17,54,57,69,79,81,83,84,85,89,103,109
Nehemiah 2:4 8, 106
nest, 2, 140
net, 9,
nevertheless, 72
nigh, 91
night, 7,10,19,78,85
Nimrod, 1
Noah, 119,120
Noe, 19
noise, 8, 25
none, 21,61,69,72,73,139
non-Christians, 31,82
north, 1, 87,140
nostrils, 120
notable, 86
nothing, 1,96,125
notwithstanding, 14, 107
nought, 96
Number, 73,80
Numbers 16:6-8 124
Numbers 16:11, 125
Numbers 16:18, 125

Numbers 16:20-21, 125
Numbers 16:26-27, 125
Numbers 16:30-32, 125
Numbers 16:33-35, 126
Numbers 23:19, 133

O generation, 81,141
O inhabitant, 77
O Israel, 18
O Jerusalem, 141
Obadiah, 97
Obadiah 1:4, 2, 140
obedience, 36
obedient, 68
obey, 38, 71,74
obeying, 58
oblation, 29
off, 97
offence, 73
offend, 56
offer, 78, 108
offered, 90,91,99,126,139
offerings, 28
oil, 88
old, 58,63,112,113,120,140
olives, 87,91
Olivet, 86

once, 65
one, 18, 19,20,29,31,36,46,56,68,74,75,88,89,99,146
only, 62
open, 7,42,50,89,107,128
opened, 16,28,78,103,125
ordained, 46,86
order, 23
ought, 65
ourselves, 75
out, 13,14
outer, 20,56,106
outwardly, 126
over, 80,101
overcharged, 60
overcomes, 77,83,103,108
overcome,13,67,79,80,83,101,103, 109
overtake, 57,
own, 23,129

pains, 15
par, 28
parable, 89
paradise, 34,46,54,89,122
part, 21,30,41,45,54,126,128,140
parted, 4, 5,53
pass,8,25,53,60,85,97,121,128
133,137

passed, 36,58,63,74,94
passing, 34
passion, 49,52
pasture, 62
patience, 29,61,70,77,101,128
134
patriarch, 94,112
Paul, 35,52,132
peace, 6, 53,57,61,67,71,102,105,117, 130,135
pearls, 8
people, 46,69,71,80,82,84,118,121,126
139,140
perceiving, 18
perfect, 13,33,43,45,47,57,61,64
65,72,107,110,119,122
perfectly, 57,133
period, 13
pernicious, 127
perplexed, 113
perplexity, 89
perform, 63,126
performed, 133
perish, 2,25,39,109,129,130
perished, 22, 43, 126
persecution, 64, 68, 75
persecuted, 97
perseverance, 135
person, 94

Peter, 52, 59
1 Peter, 1:11, 65
1 Peter 1:22-23, 58
2 Peter 2:1, 142
2 Peter 2:2-3, 126
2 Peter 2:3, 126
2 Peter 2:6-7, 121
1 Peter 2:9, 66
1 Peter 2:22, 66
1 Peter 3:17-18, 65
1 Peter 4:7, 11, 24, 26, 92
1 Peter 4:12, 77
2 Peter 2:2, 127
2 Peter 2:4, 73, 143
2 Peter 2:9, 134
2 Peter 3:8-9, 25
1 Peter 4:5,   27, 46, 96, 115
1 Peter 4:7, 41, 114
Pharisees, 35, 81, 141
philosophy, 139
Philip, 34, 52, 113
Philippians 1:20, 96
Philippians 1:21, 75, 76, 84
Philippians 1:22, 112
Philippians 1:29, 64, 68, 75
Philippians 2:10, 65
Philippians 3:20-21, 14, 121
pierced, 25

pillar, 108
pit, 125,126,128,140
place, 32,54,102,107,120,121,130, 140
plagues, 15,31,100
plains, 121
planted, 19
please, 95,97,132,133
pleased, 58
pleasures, 84,117
polygamists, 126
portion, 31, 88, 89
possesses, 14,73
possessed, 73
possible, 63, 126
position, 73
pour, 28
poured, 30, 70, 100
power, 2, 4,10,12,13,19,21,23,31,39,40,
41,42,44,53,55,58,62,67,80,87,96, 100,
101,103,118,119,122
practices, 126
praise, 92
pray, 13,14,15,37,41,57,60,124,137
prayed, 8,
prayer, 11,26,41,78,92,108,114
135
praying, 135
preach, 46,140

preaching, 22
preached, 21, 29, 42, 52, 86
preachers, 71, 120
precepts, 37,84
precious, 72,93
precludes, 3, 16
priests, 21,41,42,65,71,89
prince, 69
prepare, 32,89,107
prepared, 33, 40,110
prepared, 11,24,26,36,40,47,54,92,114
preparation, 135
presence, 122
present, 100, 109
preserve, 19,100, 121
preserved, 72, 98
prevailed, 13
prevent, 43, 114, 115
principalities, 135
prison, 113
privily, 126,142
proceeded, 91
profession, 89
profits, 53
prolongs, 130
promise, 25,96
prophesy, 118

prophets, 3,14,16,63,97,98,113,117,118, 119,126,128,129,140,141,142
prophetess, 14,29,80,86,93
proponents, 126
prosper, 133
protest, 23
prove, 64
provoke, 28, 125
Psalm 37:38, 72
Psalms 51:5, 72
Psalms, 57:5, 8
Psalms 79:2-3, 72
Psalms 89:6, 106
Psalms 89:47-48, 93
Psalms 103:11, 10
Psalms 104:12, 10
Psalms 106:35, 129
Psalms 116:15, 93
Psalms 121:3-6, 100
Psalms 83:18, 64. 93
punished, 84, 102,134
punishment, 140
pure, 58,73
purified, 58

queen, 28
quench, 135

quickens, 20,   41, 53, 111
quick, 27, 43,45,46,86,91,92,95,96,110, 114,115
quiet, 76
quickly,16,45, 47,52,70,91,92

rain, 133
rained, 19
"rape," 24
raises, 20,41,81
raised, 21,22,33,38,41,42,44,45,92,95, 115
"rapture," 1 , 3, 12,24,27,28,35,41,116,145
"raptured," 4, 116
reach, 1,
ready,13,33,42, 45,47,57,115
reap, 112
reapers, 56
reason, 127
reasoning, 18
ravening, 126
rebelled, 36
receive, 76,86,89,96
received, 6, 16,29,32,49,52,61,80,82,88,96,118
recover, 84, 102
redeemed, 79,118,123
refrained, 1
reign, 21,23,37,38,64,67,75
reigned, 16,76,81,82,94,124,137

rejoice, 92
rejoicing, 23, 34
remain, 13, 33,37,42,43,45,47,57,115
remained, 141
remember, 57,61,93
remembrance, 30
remission, 39
remnant, 73,91,123
remove, 87
renewing, 63
repentance, 25, 81
repent, 38,57,61,67,97,134
repented, 14, 15
request?, 9
require, 10,
resemble, 9
reserve, 84
reserved, 73,143
respect, 94
rest, 15,43
resurrection
18,20,21,22,23,39,41,42,44,58,59,86,94,111
rest, 9, 43
restitution, 29, 86
restore, 6,
return, 19,133
returned, 86
revealed, 19, 94

Revelation 1:7, 25
Revelation 2:2, 128
Revelation 2:4, 72, 115
Revelation 2:10, 61, 134
Revelation 2:20, 14
Revelation 2:21, 14
Revelation 2:22, 67
Revelation 3:2,13,33,42,45,47,72
Revelation 3:10, 134
Revelation 2:26, 103
Revelation 3:1, 115
Revelation 3:2, 13,24, 33
Revelation 3:3, 61
Revelation 3:10, 29,61,101
Revelation 3:11, 103
Revelation 3:12, 108
Revelation 4:1-2, 28
Revelation 5:3, 107
Revelation 5:3-4, 57
Revelation 5:13, 108
Revelation 6:9, 78
Revelation 6:17, 67
Revelation 7:3, 103,134
Revelation 7:13-6-8, 103
Revelation 7:13-14, 67,75
Revelation 7:14, 29,76
Revelation 7:14-17, 78
Revelation 8:2, 33,109

Revelation 8:3, 78, 108
Revelation 8:6, 33
Revelation 8:13, 78
Revelation 9:4, 78, 134
Revelation 9:20-21, 15
Revelation 10:7, 33
Revelation 11:3, 118
Revelation 11:7, 78
Revelation 11:11-12, 30
Revelation 11:3, 108
Revelation 12:5-6, 54
Revelation 12:7, 72, 84
Revelation 12:17, 72
Revelation 13:6-8, 103
Revelation 13:7, 13, 78, 109
Revelation 13:8, 78
Revelation 13:17, 73
Revelation 14:1, 78, 118
Revelation 14:4, 118
Revelation 14:3-4, 78
Revelation 14:1, 123
Revelation 14:4-5, 123
Revelation 14:5, 119
Revelation 14:6, 108
Revelation 14:13, 43
Revelation 15:2-3, 80
Revelation 16:6, 77
Revelation 16:17-20, 30

Revelation 16:9, 15
Revelation 16:11, 15
Revelation 16:21, 15
Revelation 16:21, 31
Revelation 17:3, 15
Revelation 17:6, 13
Revelation 17:8, 80, 118
Revelation 17:18, 80
Revelation 18:1, 108
Revelation 18:24, 14,16,68,80,118,119,124
Revelation 19:1, 80,108
Revelation 19:11, 16,90
Revelation 19:11-14, 90
Revelation 19:17, 108
Revelation 19:19, 90
Revelation 19:21, 91
Revelation 20:3, 82
Revelation 20:4, 16,70,76,80,82,118,123
Revelation 20:6,21, 59
Revelation 20:5-6, 22,38,40,44
Revelation 20:9, 16, 83
Revelation 20:10, 83
Revelation 20:14, 22,39,40,44
Revelation 21:7, 83
Revelation 21:8, 22,39,40,128
Revelation 22:7, 16
Revelation 22:12, 16, 70
Revelation 22:15, 118

Revelation 22:18-19, 133
Revelation 2:20-21, 14
revived, 95
reward, 17,27,45,87,92,97
rich, 87
riddance, 70
right, 6, 49
righteous, 11,21,36,39,41,75,102,130,138
righteousness, 16,32,39,50,59,89,90,102,130,133,138
rise, 18,22,23,24,65,66,92,111,115, 126
risen, 22,53
river, 10,
roaring, 89
robes, 29,75? 76,78
robber, 138
rod, 54
Romans 1:7, 71
Romans 2:9, 66
Romans 2:16, 44, 92
Romans 3:10, 75, 77
Romans 3:23,74, 75
Romans 5:2, 74
Romans 5:2-3,36
Romans 5:3, 36
Romans 5:12, 36, 74
Romans 5:19, 36
Romans 5:21, 37
Romans 6:6, 112

Romans 6:6-10, 38,95
Romans 6:23,38,112
Romans 7:5, 112
Romans 8:8, 112
Romans 8:13, 112
Romans, 9:27, 82
Romans 9:28, 89
Romans 10:6-7,   50
Romans 10:7, 138
Romans 11:11, 50
Romans 13:12-13, 38
Romans 16:17, 117
Rome, 71
rose, 21, 43
rudiments, 139
rule, 23, 53

Sabbath's, 86
sackcloth, 118
sacrifice, 72, 74
sacrificed, 14,29
Sadducees 17,35,41,42,44,59,81,141
safety, 57,76
saints, 8, 13,14,16,42,68,71,72,73,77,7879,80,83,93,98,103,118,119, 124,135
sake 59,60?62,63,68,70,75,99,113, 136

sanctify, 99
sanctuary, 74
sand, 82
salvation, 61,65,80,91,135,137
same 86,136,138
Sardis, 115
sat, 123
Satan 64,122,123,142
save, 19, 105
saved, 42,62,66,68,69,86,102,136,137139
Savior, 24, 92
scarcely, 39
scarlet, 15
scorch, 100
scorched, 15
scribe, 10, 18, 19, 65
scriptures, 18, 31
scorpions, 53, 101
scourge, 65, 66
sea, 80,82, 88, 89
seducing, 138
seal, 78, 79,134
sealed, 103,134
seared, 117
searching, 65
season, 83, 117
seat, 96
second 41,44,45,59,85,90,128,143

secrets, 20,43,92
security, 127
send, 86
sent, 98, 99, 121
sepulchre 53, 94, 112
seduce, 14,
seducing, 11,17
see, 15,37,50,53,55,56,57,110,113
seed 8,17,18,37,55,56,58,73,133
seeing, 121
seek, 11,13,24,26,40,47,51,58,59,62,92,110,114,140
seeking, 8,
seen 50
"seized," 5
sell, 73
send, 56
sent, 133,141
separate, 57
separated, 31, 53
serpents, 53, 101, 127
serve, 38, 74, 85, 112
serving, 84, 117
seven, 17,18,33
seventh, 30, 33
sever, 56
servants, 8, 9,14,20,31,38,56,72,80,88,89, 134
shade, 100
shake, 128

shaken, 12, 87, 128
shame, 48, 69, 85
shape, 50, 105
share, 67
shed, 72, 77
sheep, 57, 126, 138
sheepfold, 138
shepherd, 57, 138
shield, 135
shines, 88
shod, 135
shoes, 104
short, 36,75,89,93
shout, 43, 45, 92
show, 28, 33, 86
showed, 39, 53
sides, 2, 140
sight, 32, 49,72,93,104,141
sign, 12,17,63,67,86,89,126
signify, 61, 65
similitude, 105
Simon, 50, 53
Simon Peter, 59
sin, 36,37,38,39,50,62,65,66,74,75,90,91,94,94,100,101,112, 120, 125
sing, 80
sinned 36,37,70,74,75,94,95,142

sinners, 36,39,69
Sion, 79,118,123
silver, 15,70
Sir, 68, 75, 78
sit, 1, 78
sitting, 88, 119
six, 33
skin, 105
sky, 8
slack, 25
slackness, 25
slain, 14,16,68,78,79,91,97,103,118, 119,123,124
sleep 22,33,41,44,48,85,92,100,114, 115
slept, 23,42,88,90
slumber, 100,127,142
slumbered,   88,90
smite, 100
smoke, 86
snare, 60,102,128,137
'snatch' 24
"snatched, away"
snow, 133
sober, 24,26,36,40,92,115,137
Sodom, 19,121,141
somewhat, 72
sold, 19
son, 4,41,53,55,62,65,124
Son, 23, 62

song, 79 ,80
Son of God, 90
Son of man, 10,12,17,19,41,45,48,50,53,55,57,60,65,67,85,87,88,89,133, 137
soul,16,66,76,78,80,82,93,118,123,139
sound, 33,34,44,45,78,92,117
sounded, 33
south, 87, 115
sorcerers, 45, 128
sorceries, 15
sores, 15
sows, 55,112
sowed, 8, 56
sower, 133
space, 14
spared, 142
speaks 1,11,17,27,40,74, 81,94,112,128, 138, 139,141
speaking, 74
speech, 70
speedy, 70
speedily, 10
spirit, 11,17,28,30,34,43,52,107, 111,112,128,138,139
Spirit, 13,52,58,61, 135
spiritual, 135
spitefully, 65
spit, 66,94
spitted, 65

spoil, 86, 139
spoilers, 2,
spoke, 42,53,74,105,125
spoken, 29,32,117,127,140
stablish, 101
stand, 23,41,52,60,67?69,87,96,104, 135,137
standing, 48,60,108
stars, 1,9,12,55,67,87,89,141
statues, 11,24,26,36,40,47,92,110,114
steadfastly, 32
sting? 129
stone, 15,31,81,141
stood, 32,33,108,123
strait, 111
strange, 77,139,142
strength, 2, 10,106
strengthen, 13,33,42,45,47,57,96,110
stretch, 117,140
strikes, 101
strong, 4, 27,136,138
stumbled, 82
succor, 66
sudden, 57
suffered, 65,66
suffers, 14,64,65,66,67,68,70,70,98, 100,102,130
suffering, 65
subdue, 25
subdued, 23

suddenly, 52
subject, 23,96,107
sun, 19,12,67,86,87,100,108
sunder, 89
sung, 79
supplication, 135
surfeiting, 60,137
suffer, 61,66,75,136
suffering, 61
swallow, 126
sware, 68
swear, 133,137,139,141
swift, 127, 142
swollen, 52
sword, 97,123,135
sworn, 133

tabernacle, 103
talent, 31
talking, 28
take, 13,14,19,32,39,55,73,98,103, 128,135
taken, 31, 102, 129
taking, 135
tares, 56
tarried, 88, 90
tarry, 51,58,59,63,94
taste, 48,57

taught, 42
teach, 11, 14,24,26,36,40,47,
teachers, 117,127,142
tears, 78
teeth, 20,31,56,88,107
tell, 122
temple, 30, 108
temptation 29,61,62,77,84,100,102,130, 136
tempted, 62,66,102,130,136
ten, 9,15
tents, 125
test, 128
testator, 96
testified, 22, 61
testify, 46, 86
testimony, 58,73,78,79
tetrarch, 112,113
thanks, 58,129,136
thief, 25,57,60
thefts, 15
themselves 18,33,63,94,102,117,127,142
1 Thessalonians 2:15, 97
1 Thessalonians 4:16, 45
1 Thessalonians 4:17, 39,47
1 Thessalonians 4:13-17, 16,17,21,24,39
1 Thessalonians 4:15, 114
1 Thessalonians 4:14-16 42,115
1 Thessalonians 5:6, 40

1 Thessalonians 5:8, 137
2 Thessalonians 2:9, 45,127,140
2   Thessalonians 2:11, 27,28,138
2 Thessalonians 3:3, 100
till, 135
think, 74
times 11,51,105,112,127,132,140,142
1 Timothy 4:1, 11, 17
2 Timothy 2:26, 102
2 Timothy 4:1, 42,45,110
2 Timothy 4:8, 102
thee?, 59,
things, 6, 9,11,13,14,23,24,25,26,28,29, 36,41,45,46,47,49,54,58,60,61,63,67,80,89,92,111,113?1 17,123,125,130,137,140,141
third, 7, 14,46,53,66
thoughts, 101,121
thousand 16,21,25,41,70,76,81,82,83, 118,124,137
three, 30
three hundred, 4
thrice, 60,123
throne, 1, 17,28,29,30,54,78,79,82,119, 123,140
thrust, 136
thunders, 30
thyself 2,
times, 11,29,61,62,66,127,139
Titus, 84,92,117

today? 6,
together, 18,20,57,72,87,89,90,98,115, 125
took, 5,8,17,88,125
tomorrow, 24,124
tongues, 13,29,79,103,109,133
torment, 101,107
tormented, 83
tortured, 22
touch, 51,125
touching, 18
toward, 10,18,87,94
tower, 1, 69
tradition, 139
transformed, 63, 64
transforming, 63, 142
transgression, 95
translated, 4, 58
translation, 58
transportation, 11
transporter, 11
travail, 57
traveling 9
tread, 53
treasure 8,
treasurers, 10
trees, 103,134
tribes, 12,17

tribulation
12,19,116,9,20,29,36,66,67,68,71,75,76,77,84,127,143
trodden, 74
trouble, 66,69,76
troubled, 32
true, 13,80,90
True, 16
Trump, 44,45,92,115
trumpet, 28,33,44,45,69,78,92,110
trust, 73
truth, 13,37,60,62,99,127,135
try 29,61,78,134
turned, 104
twinkling, 33,44,45,92,110,115
two, 19,31,32,54,111,120
two hundred, 118
two hundred and fifty men 126

unawares, 60,137
unbelievers, 89,129
understand, 125
understanding, 142
unequally, 129
unfeigned, 58
unfruitful, 129,142
ungodly, 39,76,120,121
unjust 19,42,65,84,94

unjustly, 39,86
unmovable, 136
unprofitable,   20,56,88
upright, 122
uprightness, 39
unrighteousness, 37,38
unspeakable, 34,46,90,122
us-ward, 25
unwise, 142
utter, 35, 46,122
utterance, 135
Uz, 122

vain, 22,77,93? 129,136
valley, 3,87
vanity, 130
vapor, 86
vessels, 88
vesture, 90
vexed, 121
vial, 30,100
victory, 129?136
virgins, 9,79,123
vile, 24
vipers, 35,39,67,81,141
visions, 10,53,54,74,122,129
visited, 39

voice, 20,28,30,43,51,68,92,105,108,111, 115
voices, 30,78
void, 133

wages, 38,112
wail, 25
wait, 136
walk, 15
walked, 4, 119
wall, 127
war, 13,16,63,73,77,90,109
warned, 36,39,81
warning, 6
washed, 29,68,76,78
watch, 24,26,36,41,54,88,92,115
watching, 135
watchful, 13,33,47,57
waters, 7, 78,94,133
waves, 89
wax,   117
waxen, 120
ways, 62,127,130
weaken, 1,
wear, 13,74
wedding, 56,89
week, 29
weeping, 20,31,56,88,107

weight, 31
west, 106
whence, 24
wherefore, 135
whirlwind, 3, 5,
white, 16,29,32,68,78,90
whole, 60,71,134
whoring, 139
whoremongers, 45,118,128
wicked, 39,56,76,101,120? 130,134,136
wickedly,   36
wickedness, 101,130,135
wife, 17,18,113
wiles, 135
will, 39,41,64,108
willing, 107,109
wilderness, 38? 94
windows, 128
wings, 98
wipe, 78
wise, 27,50,88,138,139
withers, 133
withstand, 135
witness, 9,16,22,51,70,76,105,118,124,137
wives, 125
wizards, 139
woe, 78
woman, 9, 13,54,62,89,118

women, 22,28,31,53,79,80
wonders, 63,126
wood, 15,28
word, 16,37,43,46,47,76,99,102,105,115,117,125,129,130,133, 135
136,137
works, 13,17,25,43,45,47,57,87,89,92,98,103,110,112,115,128,130
workers, 63
working, 25
world 13,14,15,29,32,36,37,50,52,55,61,62,74,78,94,98,99,101, 128,132,134,140
worms, 105
worse, 117
worshippers, 13,39
worshipped,16,76,80,82,124, 137
worship, 13,15,79,103
worthy, 41,77,81
wrath, 36,39, 69,80
wrestle, 135
write, 43,108,115
written, 79,90,107,123,136
wroth, 72

X

young men, 101
years, 4, 38, 82, 118
yield, 38
yourselves, 57, 60, 81, 89, 101, 136

Zacharias 14:1, 86
Zacharias 14:8, 87
Zephaniah 1:15-17, 69
Zephaniah 1:18, 69

SOURCES

Wikipedia, the free encyclopedia,
Dictionary.com

www.ingramcontent.com/pod-product-compliance
Lightning Source LLC
Chambersburg PA
CBHW051342040426
42453CB00007B/366